Bacon & Eggs

Bacon & Eggs

✦

How to Be Totally Committed to Your Sales Career

Jim Cross

iUniverse, Inc.

New York Bloomington Shanghai

Bacon & Eggs
How to Be Totally Committed to Your Sales Career

iUniverse books may be ordered through booksellers or by contacting:

iUniverse
1663 Liberty Drive
Bloomington, IN 47403
www.iuniverse.com
1-800-Authors (1-800-288-4677)

ISBN: 978-0-595-47480-6 (pbk)
ISBN: 978-0-595-71142-0 (cloth)
ISBN: 978-0-595-91751-8 (ebk)

Printed in the United States of America

Contents

Introduction

What is your definition of commitment? How committed are you to your own success? You may think you know the meaning of commitment, but do you really? Do you have what it takes to be a winner? I will never forget the first time I heard the analogy of commitment and its association with the well-known breakfast staple, bacon and eggs. In terms of contributors, the chicken is involved, but the pig is committed! The pig gives everything of itself to the meal. In today's sales arena, there are too many chickens and not enough pigs. In order to achieve ultimate success, you can't just be involved; you have to be committed and give everything you can to your sales career, just as the pig gives its all to the bacon and eggs meal.

Bacon & Eggs touches upon the key ingredients needed for any successful sales career. It is my hope that you will make a commitment to your own success and then use the building blocks in this book to help you reach your next level.

You will find that *Bacon & Eggs* is a straightforward read with real life examples to help communicate key points. Regardless of your particular sales profession, the concepts from this book can be applied to your career. I touch upon a wide range of topics that will ultimately help you increase sales and secure stronger relationships. I have outlined subjects such as sample sales campaigns, how to ask for referrals, and time-management ideas, just to name a few. I developed my methods during the many years I spent increasing sales profits at multiple companies, both as a salesperson and manager. I have also made the principles described in this book the foundation of my consulting and training company, and now I want to share them with you.

Sales is not business, it is personal. I for one take it personally if a prospect won't buy from me. You should too. This is your livelihood. If you don't take it personally, then maybe you're in the wrong career. This book isn't about better quality of life or work-life balance. It is about making money.

Get motivated. Get focused. Get rich.

1

Commitment: The Chicken Is Involved, but the Pig Is Committed!

If you have commitment, you are way ahead of the game. If you don't, you will never be a top performer. The good news is there is help. Success is possible. I'm not talking small success; I'm talking real success. If you have commitment, you can achieve a six-figure income rather easily. If you are truly committed, then there are no limits to your income. What? Do you think I'm crazy? Do people buy what you sell? Do clients have a need for your product? If the answer is no, then do something else. If the answer is yes, then commit to your success and sell like there is no tomorrow! Houses, cars, technology, Fortune 500 software solutions, it doesn't matter. Sell it like your life depends on it! Make a commitment and achieve victory!

Commitment is the foundation of any successful person's career. It is similar to passion and attitude. When you look at an all-star athlete, executive, or the like, you will most often find that he or she has unparalleled passion for what he or she does, coupled with a positive attitude. Passion and attitude are the ingredients of commitment. Commitment is that feeling you have deep down in your gut. It is your conscience talking to you when you leave the office early. It is your gut telling you to start early and finish late. It is the trait that winners possess. Look in the mirror. Only there will you find where the buck stops. If you want something done right, take accountability and make it happen. Don't blame others and don't expect others to achieve success for you. Top performers don't make excuses; they overcome.

Your commitment, passion, and attitude will shape your future. Commitment is the promise you make to yourself that you will be successful no matter what it takes. If you have to work sixteen-hour days, you do it. If you have to work seven days a week, you do it. If you get it wrong the first time, you blame no one and you start over. Commitment is accepting responsibility for your future and dedicating yourself to your goals.

You have to be committed to your success, but you don't have to be committed to your job. Your job doesn't matter; it is simply a vehicle to achieve your personal goals and enjoy your life. Commitment to your success is self-motivated. Because this commitment is inspired internally, it is your personal passion. Think about it; people who put up huge sales numbers don't have to care about their job. For the most part, their numbers are their job. If they don't perform, they are gone. However, when they do perform, their compensation reflects their efforts accordingly, and now they are considered an asset to the company.

What about the person who is underperforming? Everyone has been around the person who drains all the energy out of the room when he or she comes into a meeting. Do you think he or she is an asset to the company? No way. This person is nothing but overhead and an HR nightmare that can't be fired. No one cares about underperformers. Underperformers care about their job because they know they aren't marketable. Top performers thrive because they are always successful. You will never find a top performer that is committed to his or her job. Top performers will always be committed to their own success. Consequently, the company will love them unless they tank. It is a selfish world.

Have you ever heard the phrase "what have you done for me lately?" That is exactly what you should be asking yourself. What have you done for your own personal fulfillment lately? If you aren't giving everything you have, then you haven't done much for yourself. If you are blaming someone else for your shortcomings, then go away. I don't want you in my readers circle. I have no time for those who can't take responsibility for their own actions. However, if you are a winner, and if you are committed to your own personal fulfillment, then let's make some money!

So how can we relate commitment to your situation? The answer is work ethic. We live in a world of a ten-hour day. That means a minimum of ten hours just to show up and get in the game. For the most part, regardless of your profession, you will find top performers working at least ten hours a day. Perhaps you will find the chosen few that have their business so streamlined that they can get by with less. But I can promise you that they didn't get there by working eight hours a day. Top performers work hard, and they do it for hours on end. They start their day before 8:00 AM, and they finish when their work is done. They may cold-call, e-mail, or do early-morning meetings, but they start productivity at 8:00 AM or earlier. Stop and think about this. They start early, and they don't finish until their work is done. They will stay and/or work as late as necessary to get in their prospect calls, mailers, follow-up calls, meetings, demos, and so on. They don't stop until their work is done.

It is my opinion that if you work harder than your peers, you will see a larger W-2 more times than not. It's okay to work smarter, but working harder is the real ingredient. Typically, you will find that these qualities are synonymous. People who care enough to work harder will also work smarter. If we assume that there are ten hours in a day, this means you are working from 8:00 AM until 6:00 PM with maximum productivity. The early bird definitely gets the worm. Water-cooler talk doesn't do you any good. It is usually just a bunch of people complaining or avoiding work. You don't need this. Your money is waiting for you on the phone and in customer meetings.

When you take lunch, make it a working lunch. Then you are back on it until your work is finished. Get the most out of your day. Don't let others drag you down. Keep your head down and make it happen.

Perhaps if I share a real-life experience it will communicate how important work ethic is and what kind of results can be achieved from dedication and commitment:

For a portion of my sales career, I was a sales rep for a Fortune 500 technology provider. It was a phone-based sales position, so most of the relationships were solidified over the phone as opposed to in person. When I was recruited to this company, they told me that the average first-year rep made in the neighborhood of fifty thousand dollars a year. This figure then jumped to around sixty-five thousand dollars the second year, and the third year typically showed one hundred thousand dollars in earnings. Upon hearing this, I figured that if an average rep was performing at these levels, then I could surely do better than average.

Every Tuesday and Thursday around 9:00 AM, co-workers would line up at the break room for the free bagels and doughnuts that the company graciously provided. One day, a peer and I approached the break room and realized that there were too many people in line and the wait would take several minutes. It would be easier just to come back later. What stuck in my mind was what my co-worker said when I asked the question, "Why do all of those reps stand in that line when they could be on the phone selling?" He responded, "Because it is easier to do nothing than to cold-call for new business." That one sentence hit me like a ton of bricks. He was spot on with his shrewdness. Anyone can do nothing, but few have the commitment to stay focused and active.

I was in sales for two years before being promoted to management. There were about ten of us who ran in the same group and shared the same work ethic. We all posted similar results and blew away the compensation averages. It came down to the fact that we worked our tails off each and every day. We were typically the first reps in the office and often the last to leave. We were doing 130 calls a day when everyone else was only doing 75. Toward the end of my sales career, I had developed a book of business that allowed me to reduce my workday from twelve hours to about nine hours.

Don't get me wrong; in no way, shape, or form am I saying that we were "better" than the other performers. We simply had the commitment and drive to take what was ours. I for one was money motivated. I only cared about the money. I wasn't doing it for the practice, and I sure wasn't doing it to impress anyone. I just wanted the money. My own self-interest was fulfilled by my commitment and dedication.

I had a VP of sales tell me one time that there was no such thing as vacation time. His point was that when a career or obtaining a goal is taken seriously, it is a 24/7 gig. It becomes part of your life. He would literally be working in some capacity every day of the week even if he was on vacation. Some would say that this type of activity is too extreme and over the top. People may even say that it is a one-way ticket to get burned out and would eventually be counterproductive. Without exploring this, on the surface, those notions would make sense. However, if we dig deeper, maybe it will become a little clearer that those perceptions aren't necessarily correct.

This particular person would regularly send e-mails late at night, and it wasn't uncommon to see correspondence from him on the weekends as well. On occasion I would even get calls at my house on a Saturday or Sunday. While he took "vacation," he would call into the office probably once or twice a day. This type of behavior may seem a bit much to most people, but it isn't out of line for someone who is truly committed to his or her success. Remember, we aren't talking about making minimum wage here. We are talking about very high incomes. In order to achieve these incomes, one has to be fully committed and prepared to handle the responsibilities that are required of those at the top.

He would balance his time so that he could be with his family and also take care of his career goals. He took care of his priorities. The trade-off for his commitment was a handsome salary and security for him and his family. He knew what he wanted and did what he had to do in order to make it happen. He never quit and never let up. Of course it would be great to be able to turn off and shut down each day at closing time, but that simply isn't possible when it comes to this level of play. If it was easy, anyone could do it. He knew what was in store when he decided that he wanted to be successful. When he committed to his success, he knew that there would be long hours and pressure.

Think of the above example and its comparison to the life of a professional athlete. Do you think an athlete's work stops when the season is over? Of course not. During the off-season, pro athletes have to continue rigorous training regiments and watch their diet seven days a week. They don't simply stop because it is Saturday or they are on vacation. I can only imagine what it would be like for NFL players. They have games on Sunday coupled with classroom work and practice all week. When they get home, they are still mentally preparing for the next game. During the off-season, they have to stay in shape and continue to work on the core components of their game. They can relax when they retire.

Once you can make the vow to truly commit yourself to your own success, you will start to see things a little differently. The sales trainings won't seem as boring because you will be looking for something you can use in order to increase your numbers. You may even go as far as to subscribe to monthly trade publications in order to better educate yourself in your particular field. Perhaps you will pick up the paper and review the business section with a newfound interest. Maybe you will devote one Saturday a month to researching new leads. All of these things are part of the commitment process. You have to always be pushing to make yourself better and constantly raising your own bar. Do the best you can, plus a little more.

2

Activity: Get in the Game!

From a management standpoint, it is very frustrating to have a rep drown in a strategic-planning period. The failure happens because of too much talking and not enough doing. Having been in management and sales, I have seen both sides of the fence. In the end, the managers or reps that simply generate activity will ultimately prevail. The ones that continue to think and re-think their ideas will be left behind.

I was in a meeting with a technology partner discussing a new offering that the partner wanted to bring to market. Out of respect for the person that arranged the meeting, I was prepared to give him as much time as he wanted. After initial introductions, we got down to the business of discussing the product and its functionality in the marketplace. It wasn't a difficult concept. I asked a couple clarifying questions and was able to grasp the idea in about ten minutes. So the total meeting time up to this point had been approximately fifteen minutes.

I could have walked out of the meeting at that point and had no problem whatsoever implementing his solution. I even verbally said, "Okay, it makes sense. I got it." He proceeded to waste another hour and forty-five minutes of my time with PowerPoint presentations and meaningless gibberish. The only reason I let it go as long as it did is because I knew I could use it as leverage the next time I needed a favor from the meeting organizer. I wanted to scream from the top of my lungs, "Guys, this isn't that difficult! In the amount of time you have already wasted, we could have called fifteen customers and possibly made a sale!"

The above example is not all that uncommon in today's sales arena. Reps and managers spend way too much time planning and not enough time executing. I have seen planning sessions that ran for three months at a time. Are you kidding me? By the time they figure out what they want to do, the competition has probably already closed a deal. There is obviously a need to have some sort of plan before you proceed with your offering. But you shouldn't drown in details and red tape. Get in the game and do something!

Note to managers: If you have to continually revisit strategic planning sessions with your people, then you have the wrong people. If your team can't execute a simple concept in a timely fashion, get new people.

Note to sales reps: If you can't immediately get in front of customers to implement applicable ideas, then quit wasting everyone's time. Get out of sales and do something else.

Let's use a hypothetical example from the real estate industry:

The managing broker calls a lunch meeting for all the agents. The topic of discussion is increasing residential housing sales through a campaign focusing on homeowners insurance. The idea is to offer up a promotion that the real estate agent will buy the new residents homeowners insurance for the next year if they close on a home by XYZ date. Perhaps you have some sort of parameters such as "not to exceed X amount of dollars." But the idea is very simple: If you buy your house from me by XYZ date, I will pay for your homeowners insurance for the next year.

That's it. It is simple. You make sure that your commissions cover the costs of the insurance and also put a little money in your pocket. You set the parameters accordingly. Maybe you have a minimum purchase price, or maybe you have to be the listing agent as well as the selling agent. You evaluate your potential risks, then you overcome those challenges, and then you execute the plan. Done.

A top rep will grasp this and run with the concept immediately. A skeptic will challenge the idea and poke holes in the concept. He or she will say things like: "What if our commissions don't cover the insurance?" "Why would we make an offer like this?" "Doesn't this seem like buying the business?" "I'm not sure if this is ethical." While these people are making excuses, the top performers have already formulated a plan and are most likely putting it into action.

My response to people who question new ideas is: "It is a promotion. It is an idea. It is a concept. X percent of zero is zero. If you don't sell a house by XYZ date, there are zero commissions to be paid out. I am simply giving you an idea that may help you sell more homes in a short time frame. You either get it or you don't. Quit fighting ideas that are trying to help you and just get to work. Take the concept and tailor it to your own style, but get in the game and do something! Make something happen; don't sit on the sidelines and watch. Offer up ten free tickets for a lawn-care service, but just do something—anything! In general, negative people look for ways to question ideas when they could simply give them a try and see what happens. Don't get bogged down questioning every new or unusual idea without taking any action.

Activity is the key. If you want to achieve your fullest potential, then you have to be doing something. Regardless of your profession, the formula is fairly constant. Always be contacting prospects and existing customers. You should be talking to people morning, noon, and night. You should be setting up face-to-face meetings, conference calls, product demos, and so on, every single day. It doesn't matter if your plan is bulletproof. Just get in front of the customer and get something going. E-mails and collateral material can give you a reason to call, but they are definitely not the sole answer. You can't hide behind e-mails and marketing information. You have to roll up your sleeves and get involved.

Set stretch goals for yourself with face-to-face meetings. If you have only been hitting six meetings a week, try to stretch it to nine. Three extra meetings a week gives you roughly one hundred fifty extra meetings a year. You can't tell me something good wouldn't happen out of an extra one hundred fifty meetings a year. If you have only been making ten new prospect calls a day, bump it up to fifteen. This will give you one thousand two hundred fifty extra calls in a year's time. If you have three lines on your phone, figure out a way to use them all. They are not there to simply take up space. You may think I am kidding, but I couldn't be more serious.

Let me give you another example: When I was in the tech industry, my job often involved conference calls with existing clients, me, and a potential vendor. We all know how frustrating it is to set up conference calls. It typically involves a bunch of e-mails and voice mails to nail down a time. In reality, all we really need is maybe three minutes of the person's time to see if there is interest. If there is interest, the clients will most likely stay on the phone much longer than three minutes.

When I had an idea or offering that was worth positioning to my clients, I would have the vendor hold on the second line, and I would do a call blast of maybe ten potential contacts. As soon as I got the customer on the phone, I would give a quick pitch that outlined why I was calling and then ask if I could conference in the vendor that was holding on the other line. Assuming I had a solid relationship with the account, the customers were typically okay talking shop with the vendor. They would get involved with technical speeds and feeds and other relevant information. I would put them on hold (the hold music didn't interfere when I was in conference mode), let them talk shop, and make another couple calls on my third line. Maybe I would set up some more meetings or carry out other business.

The point is that I was offering my client a value add with my vendor, and I was also prospecting and contacting new customers all at the same time. I had three lines and I used them. Try it sometime; you will be exhausted at the end of the day. That's when you know you did your best. For those of you who say, "Yeah, but I feel like I should be on the phone managing the call as opposed to dumping it on the vendor," you need to have an open mind for ideas like this. If something like this is out of your comfort level, then mold it to something that fits your style.

One way that may help you increase your activity is to develop a touch campaign. I would start by breaking out the top accounts that you are focusing on and then add a few prospects to the list. Write out a plan of action that will allow you to touch each account in some fashion at least once a week. The challenging part will be coming up with relevant reasons as to why you are contacting them. You have to make sure your touches offer value to the client and also satisfy your goals of advancing the relationship.

If you do choose to go with a touch campaign, you have to hold yourself accountable at the end of each week. It is a waste of time to put forth the effort of coming up with the plan if you never do anything with it. Perhaps you can put something together that focuses on various components that are critical to the success of your business. For example, your plan could involve net-new clients, new offerings with existing clients, and maintenance of customer service levels. You can then apply that plan across your account/client base.

It may be beneficial to you if you break your account base up into thirds. The top tier can be the most profitable accounts based on existing spending and/or potential. The second tier would be midrange clients that are not huge in potential but are there for you day in and day out. And lastly, your bottom tier could be those accounts that do not necessarily have low potential but perhaps require long-term commitment levels. The bottom tier may be the whale that everyone is looking to land, but realistically speaking it will take a long time to get the business.

Once you have the general plan in place, the next part is simple execution to hit your goals. You may have to extend the length of your workday in order to accomplish all of the items on your to-do list, but in the end you will see an increase in your business. Increasing your activity level is a great way to generate more sales.

Stop making excuses and just get in the game.

3

Referrals: I'm Not Doing This for the Practice!

Everyone talks about referrals, but few actually pursue them. Referrals should be considered the reward for a job well done. They are the by-product of your excellent customer service. As a true sales professional, you have earned the right to ask for and receive referrals. If you are not asking for referrals, you are only cheating yourself. Earning referral business is a fantastic way to grow your business, and the best part is that all of the calls are warm leads.

There are two main types of referrals:

- Client to Client
- Client to Co-worker (in-house hand-off)

Both of these offer a plethora of untapped sales opportunities. The hardest part is actually asking for the referral. Sometimes it may seem pushy, or we may be fearful that we haven't earned the right to ask for referrals. Maybe we simply have forgotten about the idea. Let's discuss a few of the best ways to ask for the referral, and then we will break down each type for further review.

The referral concept is one of those areas where you absolutely need to have a game plan and well-thought-out strategy. Think about what you are doing: you are asking someone to put his or her neck out on the line and jeopardize his or her reputation by recommending you to another client or co-worker. The concept of "ready, aim, fire" should not be used. You get one or maybe two chances to do this the right way, so be prepared. Most importantly, be professional.

If at all possible, it is best to approach this topic after your client has successfully implemented your product. Also, keep in mind that your client is extremely busy. It is better to venture into this area after the close of their quarter, project, or general busy time. Yes, everyone is busy, but there are peak times when it is best not to push too hard. In general, try to hit them up for a referral when things are going smoothly.

View the referral concept as you would any other sales pitch. You are pitching the client on giving you a referral. With this being said, you don't just say, "Hey can you give me some referrals?" If it were that easy, we could simply say, "Hey will you buy from me?" You need to show why you have earned the right to a referral. You need to present the hard work and excellent customer service you have given the client over the past X months. You need the client to understand that you are the greatest thing since the invention of the wheel. He or she should want to refer you to other contacts.

The overall idea is to have a review session with your client that initially takes care of his or her needs and then allows you a transition into your needs (referrals). I would first start out by asking the customer for a lunch meeting or perhaps a conference call to review his or her account and get an overall status check of where he or she stands with everything. During this time, you need to literally present the client with something tangible or electronically viewable, such as customer service reports, product breakdowns, returns, or project deadlines. It doesn't really matter what you present as long as it makes you look good and will be viewed in a positive light by the client. You need something to get him or her thinking, "Yes, I have been very pleased over the past three months."

In all seriousness, if you have been holding up your end of the bargain, then this should be easy for you to present. If you can't present a favorable overview, then you most likely haven't earned the right to ask for referrals. Make sure your client is satisfied and happy with your service. Your presentation should be structured and professional. It is okay to do it over lunch, but make sure the client knows that you are taking this seriously. During your presentation, you have to communicate three things to the customer:

1.   You and the client agreed upon X.

2.   You delivered X.

3.   The client is happy with X.

Here is a sample dialogue:
Sales Rep:
"Mrs. Customer, I wanted to take this opportunity to thank you for your business and get a feel for how things have been going over the past few months. I have prepared a detailed report outlining our most recent project and the applicable high points within the project. As we discussed, you wanted XYZ implementation to be up and running by XYZ date. As you can see, we came in ahead of schedule and under budget.

"Also, you said it was imperative that there were no glitches with this implementation, and it was crucial that everything was running smoothly by your busy season. Unless there is something I am not aware of, everything seems to be running smoothly, and the project has been delivered without a flaw.

"With this being said, how would you rate your overall satisfaction with our most recent project?"
Client:
"We are extremely happy with the implementation and look forward to working with you in the future."
Sales Rep:
"I echo your sentiments of working together on future projects. Mrs. Customer, I do my best to communicate clearly, deliver on expectations, and ensure that my clients are given excellent customer service. I know that you have been in the

industry for X years and that your peers and colleagues respect you. Based on my proven track record, do you feel that I have earned the right to ask you for some referrals?"

You are not doing this for the practice! You are here to make money! If you have held up your end of the bargain, then don't be afraid to ask for a bigger piece of the pie. You said you were going to do X, you did X, and the customer is happy. It is okay to ask for referrals, and your clients understand that finding new business is part of what you do. Your clients probably encourage the reps in their companies to do the exact same thing. Asking for referral business is part of the process. It is okay to ask for referral business. Let's take a look at how this concept should be applied to the two types of referrals.

Client to Client

The client-to-client referral allows you the leeway to take care of the personal interest of your existing customer. A client-to-client referral is typically a referral to someone that is outside of your customer's company—perhaps an associate in the same field but employed at different company. It is okay to offer up some sort of reward for a lucrative referral. I have seen some sales reps who have a monetary amount that they simply pay to the client for referring them to new customers. They may have a minimum purchase requirement or similar standard, but the general idea is if they get some business from the new client, they will send a referral bonus to the person who helped them. Conversely, you often can simply get the referral because your existing customer respects you and doesn't expect anything in return.

Upon making your introduction to the new client, you have to immediately let them know that you have a successful relationship with the mutual contact, and that based on your past success, the mutual contact suggested you give them a call. It has to be clear that you are calling to earn business based on your previous achievements with the mutual contact. This not only breaks the ice by having a name to drop, but it lets the new client know that you are not calling just to talk. You are calling with the purpose of getting in the loop and earning business. They will thank you for not wasting their time with a bunch of meaningless chitchat.

I trust that if you care enough about your sales career to be reading this book, you are sharp enough to be prepared when you call and meet with the new client. Don't show up expecting to have business handed to you. Remember, your old client's reputation is on the line. You not only have to impress the new client, but you have to make your old client proud and confident in his or her decision to give you the referral. Be eager and confident. Be humble and honored to have the opportunity to earn the new client's business. Be knowledgeable of his or her industry and business model. Most importantly, be professional and respectful.

Don't talk about details regarding your other client except the professional relationship you have. If you start dropping stories about going out for drinks and lavish dinners, it only makes you look foolish, and such behavior also shows that you can't keep your mouth shut. Breaking the ice doesn't mean you have to be anything other than professional.

Once you have established some rapport with the new client, it is up to you to keep the relationship alive and thriving. A referral simply allows you an opportunity to get your foot in the door, and the rest is up to you. You can't expect someone to buy from you simply because he or she met with you. You have to show credibility and earn his or her trust just like with any new account.

Client to Co-worker

This isn't that much different than the client-to-client referral, but it requires a little more hand-holding. You can't offer up a bonus incentive because it could be a conflict of interest. Your goal is to have your client champion you into other departments of his or her company based on the added value you bring to the table. Remember, if you have been holding up your end of the bargain, your client should want to have you working with the other departments and contacts.

Use the same concept as we outlined before: you agreed on X, you delivered X, and the client is happy. "Based on this proven track record, do you feel okay with me offering my services to other areas of your company?"

Lunch meetings or joint conference calls are a great way to do the introductions. If you can't get either of those, you can always settle for an e-mail with you being cc'd. Approach these referrals the same way you would approach the client-to-client referral. Make sure you are on your game and prepared to put your best foot forward.

Something to keep in mind when thinking about referrals is that it doesn't always have to be sales related. The concept of referrals is simply you proving yourself and earning the right to ask for something in return. You can prove yourself without the customer even making a purchase. If you have bent over backwards to get them information and product demos, you have still accomplished the three criteria: you agreed on X, you delivered X, and the client was happy with X. Even if they haven't purchased anything from you, you have still executed on the agreed-upon expectations. You kept your word and delivered what was wanted. This can apply to anything. It shows that you are dependable, and they can count on you.

Also, referrals don't have to be to a new contact. You can use the referral concept to expand your offerings within the same contact. If you have accomplished the three criteria, then you have earned the right to ask for other business from the same contact. This is your own way of referring yourself into net-new business with existing contacts. If you haven't given them a reason to doubt you, then why wouldn't they give you a shot at more of their business?

For example, maybe if you are a in the real estate business and have been working with a residential home buyer with continued success, it may be time to talk to this buyer about purchasing commercial property. If you are good at what you do, then you will continue to make money for your client, which ultimately means more money in your pocket. He or she should trust your professional opinion and be willing to invest in a more expensive property.

Referrals should be viewed as the low-hanging fruit when it comes to increasing your business. You completely take cold calls out of the equation and basically have the best introduction to a new opportunity that you can ask for. You are having someone refer you into new business based on his or her past satisfaction levels with your service. In theory, you should be able to double your account list simply by asking each one of your existing accounts for a referral.

Lastly, always remember to thank your client for any successful referrals. It is just common courtesy to thank someone for a referral, regardless of the outcome. You will lose credibility very quickly if you forget to thank your existing clients for their helping hand.

4

Relationships: Do What's Right, Not What's Easy!

Who would you rather buy from, someone you get along with or someone you don't? Who would you rather sell to, someone you get along with or someone you don't? These are pretty straightforward questions, but why does it seem that people have a hard time grasping this concept? Do you think your clients want a stressful relationship with someone they are giving money to?

Think about it: what can you possibly gain by constantly going against the grain and complicating the relationship with your clients? They are giving you money; you should make them want to give you more money. If they cringe every time they talk to you, I would suspect that you are close to losing them as clients. Conversely, if your clients view you as a trusted advisor, then they will automatically think of speaking with you before they make any noteworthy decisions. After we look at what it means to put your best foot forward, we will explore how to establish a solid working relationship with your clients.

Have you ever thought about what your customers think of you as a person? Do they associate you with success, or do they think you are average at best? Do they respect you and view you as a sharp individual, or do they just think of you as someone who takes care of their orders? It is very important that your image is viewed as professional and successful. Your clients will gravitate to success, as opposed to mediocrity.

I am not saying that you should drive a one-hundred-thousand-dollar car and wear a five-thousand-dollar suit. However, you should always present yourself in a successful manner, and your appearance should portray success. Think about it: if you don't look like you take care of yourself, why would customers think you can take care of their business? If you dress like a slob, then why would you pay attention to detail when it comes to your customers' needs? If you look successful and present yourself as a winner, your clients will notice. Be conservative, but don't be cheap. Be confident, but don't be arrogant. If nothing else, you at least owe your clients the respect to look professional. After all, they are the ones responsible for your income; it is important that we never lose sight of the fact that our livelihood is dependent on our clients.

Do you know why I like to pay thirty-five dollars for a haircut at a salon as opposed to fifteen dollars at a low-cost chain? I view the salon stylist as a true career professional, and I have confidence in the salon stylists to take care of me. I know that they take their career seriously, and I feel comfortable in their place of business. I look to them for advice and trust their opinion. On the other hand, I don't have that same comfort level with the less-expensive establishments. I will give you a real-life example that will bring all of this together:

I was preparing to leave on business. I realized that I was going to be on the road for about two weeks and should probably get a haircut before leaving. Unfortunately, because it was last minute, I wasn't able to get in to my normal place and had to quickly search for a last-minute replacement. This really bothered me because I liked my normal place. I felt great whenever I was there. Everyone was courteous and very polished. They always greeted me with a smile, they played music, they called me by my first name, they served me cold drinks, and they actually talked to me and truly paid attention to what I was saying. They had their act together, and I trusted them.

So out I went in search of a last-minute replacement. What I found was a fifteen-dollar haircut. The employees were all dressed in sloppy clothes, no one was talking to the clients, there wasn't any music playing, and the worst part was that no one had an up-to-date hairstyle! Are you kidding me? All of the stylists had their hair in a ponytail or were sporting something from ten years ago. Now don't get me wrong, I am not a fashion expert, but if your career is being a hairstylist, then shouldn't you at least have a decent hairstyle and look the part? Once they got me in the chair, it was like an assembly line started up. They zipped me and flipped me. I quickly paid for my shearing and went on my way vowing never to come back.

What can we learn from the above example? Image is important. I am sure that each location's skill set was very similar, and to be truthful, the fifteen-dollar haircut wasn't all that bad. (It wasn't as good as the thirty-five-dollar cut, but it wasn't a disaster either.) But the image of the thirty-five-dollar salon is what keeps me coming back. I like giving them my money. I enjoy doing business with them. I feel confident in their staff and recommendations.

Now that we look good, we can start building the relationships.

So let's face the facts: there are buyers, and there are sellers. The better the two get along, the better it is for everyone. This doesn't mean that we have to be best buddies, but it does mean that we owe it to ourselves to find some sort of common ground. We have all heard of the Golden Rule, right? It basically means, "treat people the way you want to be treated." These are words to live by. It means when dealing with customers that you do what's right, not what's easy. The best way to establish a solid relationship with a new or existing client is to treat them right! Do you like it when you call someone and get voice mail? No, so make sure you pick up your client's call if you see it coming in. Do you like waiting for two or three days to receive information? No, so make sure you provide a timely response to your client. Do you like not knowing what's going on? No, so make sure you keep your clients in the loop, even if it means giving them bad news. Don't hide behind e-mail and voice mail; do what's right, not what's easy!

In addition to doing the right thing, we also need to realize that our clients are people just like us. This means that they have hobbies and areas of interest outside of work. We need to be careful not to pry too deeply, but it is important that we take an interest in our customers' personal motivators. I'm not saying that you have to host a backyard barbeque for your customer, but in all seriousness, you should at least care about your client's personal interests. It just makes the overall relationship more personable and enjoyable for both sides. Your client will appreciate the fact that you care. It is just another way of treating people the way you want to be treated.

I will give you an example of what I mean:

I had a new account that I began working around September. It was a brand new customer, and I had no prior relationship with the account. My first call was simply an introductory call. I wanted to let the individual know that I was in the game and would be calling on him in an effort to earn his business. I sent him some information and followed up a week later. During this time, I made my intentions crystal clear: I wanted to establish a working relationship with his company that would allow me an opportunity to prove myself. At the same time, I also wanted to learn how he liked to do business and get to know him a little better.

I quickly found out that my contact was a "no nonsense" type of individual. The turning point came when I said, "Okay, I think I have a grasp of what you are looking for out of a vendor. So, what do you like to do when you're not a work?" He was taken a little off guard until I reminded him of my two initial goals: establish a working relationship and getting to know him a little better. The client told me that he played in a band. Long story short, we hit it off and I secured a very large order in October. The customer gave me a copy of the band's CD and also e-mailed me a link to their Web site. We had established a common ground outside of work. We got to know each other outside of the regimented buyer-seller relationship.

I make it a point to know all of my clients outside of the normal working relationship. Some relationships are better than others, but overall I do my best to let my clients know I am a human being just like them. It is simply easier to do business when there is a cordial working relationship. It actually creates an enjoyable buying/selling process. I have several clients who I have known for many years, and we eventually became friends more than "client/vendor."

Finding a common ground isn't really that difficult if you don't mind putting forth a little effort. Maybe your client is a baseball fan. It is fairly easy to check out the sports scores or research current activity for their favorite team. You would be surprised by the positive impact you can make by e-mailing them a recent article regarding their favorite sports team. Whatever your client's interests, it isn't that difficult to find something to talk about.

Perhaps your client wants to keep the relationship strictly business-oriented. Respect their wishes, but find ways of breaking the ice and showing you actually care about them. Maybe you can send them articles about their particular profession coupled with a handwritten note: "Tom, I saw this article on XYZ and thought you may want to take a look. Let me know if you want to grab lunch next week." The simple fact that you actually made the effort to do something like this will go a long way in building the relationship.

I never pried too much with my clients. However, I always listened for information such as dates of their birthday, maybe the anniversary of when they started with the company, or when the kids were graduating college. Depending on the situation, I would send them a simple note wishing them a happy birthday or maybe congratulating them on their five-year anniversary with the company. It was just a nice way of showing I cared.

Relationships are the lifeblood to any book of business. The stronger your relationships, the more likely you are to increase your margins and sales. When you truly are viewed as an extension of your client's work force, then you have earned the right to make a little extra money. It is important that I am clear with this point: clients value a solid working relationship. They know that you have to make money in your career. As long as you are fair, then your client understands that your services may be a little higher than your competitor. Low performers usually lead with price as their way of getting business because they have nothing else to offer. Your clients will pay a little more because of the peace of mind they get from dealing with you. You will also lose fewer clients because of the strong personal relationships you build with your accounts.

You are ultimately responsible for building the bridge that will create either a mediocre relationship or one that is strong enough to stand the test of time. How your clients perceive you is your choice. I urge you to look at each of your accounts and evaluate each individual relationship within those accounts. You never know—if you have strong enough relationships, you may be flying on the company's private jet one day.

5

Utilizing Static Information: Be Creative!

We have all had those challenging accounts that are difficult to penetrate. Our sales campaigns have stretched to over a year, and we have gotten nowhere with the potential client. Sometimes we may be lucky enough to actually secure some sort of activity, but in general the account simply isn't going anywhere. It can be very frustrating. So we have to ask ourselves if we want to continue down our existing path or maybe look at some ways of changing it up a bit.

I am always looking at ways to overcome the worst-case scenario. I do this because, if I can get through the most challenging situations, then I will triumph more times than not in the normal situations. We can't make our customers buy from us. However, we don't have to let them control our tenacity. This chapter will look at ways of using static information to help us achieve our goals.

"They are buying from me; they just don't know it yet." If you can grasp this concept, then you will prevail. Remember, we can't make them buy from us, but they can't control our tenacity. So if the account refuses to play ball, then what can we do about it? First of all, we need to look at any and all information that is available to us and realize that we aren't going to get a lot of help from our prospect. Secondly, we need to use this information in some fashion to achieve an applicable goal. You don't always have to measure success by securing an order. If you are digging in and working a difficult account, success may be defined by securing a face-to-face meeting or other small victories.

With today's technology and Internet searches, we can secure a lot of information. In addition to this, we most likely have historical data in an account that we can evaluate.

Here are a few examples of types of information we can find on our own:

- Old quotes/proposals
- Contacts
- Billing information/accounts payable
- Account address
- Recent news articles
- Stock symbols/public company information
- Company size and company vertical
- Remote locations or affiliate companies

Remember, if you don't use this information, then it is a waste of our time to even look it up. Make sure that you put it to good use. Let's briefly look at these areas and entertain possible ways to utilize them.

Old Quotes/Proposals

Have you quoted the prospect? If you haven't, then how about sending them a proactive, unsolicited quote? You don't need to wait for the client to ask you for a quote; create your own opportunity by sending a proactive quote or proposal. If there are old quotes available for viewing, see if the contact information is different from the person you have been engaging.

Contacts

Are there any old contacts listed on the account other than the person or persons that have been telling you no? If so, then why not call them to see what you can uncover? Maybe you can secure a lunch meeting with a low-level contact. If you don't have any old contacts, perhaps you can take a look at ways to uncover new contacts. For example, let's say you are in the medical supplies business and the purchasing agent has been giving you a hard time. Why not bypass the purchasing agent and actually get in touch with the people that use the supplies you are selling? Try a nurse or radiology contact. All you need is to get inside the account, and you will eventually find success.

Billing Information/Accounts Payable

I love this one. It is a great way to get contact information and find out the real players in the account. It is also the most overlooked pathway into an account. All of our accounts have some sort of accounts payable department. It is easier to get past a gatekeeper and into the accounts payable division than it is to be transferred to a high-ranking executive on a cold call. Once you get to accounts payable, let them know who you are and what you are doing. Most importantly, you need to offer some value to the AP person. For example, you can tell them that you are new to the account, and as a way to kick off the relationship, you would like to extend them Net Forty-Five terms. (Most companies expect their clients to pay their bills in 30 days as opposed to 45 days.) At the same time, you would like to confirm with whom you should actually be speaking in order to sell your product. AP people don't get a lot of sales calls; they may be more willing to give out information. You can even go as far as telling the AP person that you will be stopping by to drop them off some information regarding your company. Once they meet with you, you can most likely get a warm introduction to the "real" contact who has been avoiding you.

Account Address

This tactic is pretty simple. If they aren't coming to you, then you need to go to them. What you do once you get there is up to you. Maybe you can drop off some information at the front desk. Maybe you can have the front desk actually call down your applicable prospect. Perhaps you can see where the "after-work hangout" is and make it a point to be there once in a while. You would be amazed at the information you can pick up when people are out of the office.

Recent News Articles

Always be searching for recent articles on your accounts. You can find new contact names from people who have been quoted in the article. Once you get these names, you can call or e-mail them with a precursor of "I saw your quote in XYZ." You can also use the recent articles to gain bonus points with your existing contacts. Send them a handwritten note via U.S. Mail with the attached article (this way they can't delete your e-mail). Consider a friendly greeting, such as, "Hey Bill, great quarter for XYZ."

Stock Symbols/Public Company Information

Public companies are very easy to research. You can have information e-mailed to you anytime there is news posting for a stock symbol. You can look at the company's financial numbers and also find out the majority of the key players from its annual report. Use this information to your advantage when you contact them. Your approach could sound something like, "John, I see that you are forecasting unprecedented growth for next year. I have a solution in mind that will …"

Company Size and Company Vertical

Companies always want to know what their competitors or other companies similar to theirs are doing to better themselves. If you are able to find out the size of a company, and can bundle this information with facts about their industry, you have potential value to offer.

(It's not that hard to discover a company's size. If all else fails, drive by its location and look at the number of cars in the parking lot.) For example, if your contact is still telling you no, what do you think the CEO or CFO would do if you presented them with something that would better their company based off of your data? Try an informative and helpful approach, such as, "John, I wanted to let you know that the industry is seeing a lot of activity from companies of your size and focus. We are seeing a trend of XYZ. A few of your competitors have already started rolling out similar programs. I am including these articles that cite my examples, and I have also included a proactive proposal from my company for such-and-such solution. When can we meet to discuss this further?"

Remote Locations or Affiliate Companies

Always be looking for opportunities at other locations. This is another area that is often overlooked. If you find yourself getting in a rut at a particular location, then look for opportunities or information at their branch offices. You would be surprised by what you will find when you get outside of headquarters.

Breaking into those hard-to-penetrate accounts is not an easy task. It takes persistence and creativity. You have to be prepared to dig in for the long haul and simply never give up. The payoff is that once you do get in the loop, the hard work will have been well worth it.

The general idea is to be creative when you are working an account that is difficult to penetrate. There are many ways to measure success in terms of setting small goals. As long as you keep moving forward with baby steps, you will eventually secure an order.

6

Steps to Success: Walk Your Way to the Top!

When looking at a typical account base or book of business, one of the most common gaps I see revolves around the organizational chart. It seems that once an account has been secured, the sales rep will often times become very comfortable with whoever is giving them the business and neglect the other levels of the company. Conversely, I also see reps put on blinders when working an account for new business, and they forget that there are multiple contact levels for them to prospect. True success can be achieved once all levels of the organizational chart have been covered.

This chapter focuses on working an organizational chart at each level. I use a staircase to illustrate a typical buying situation or customer scenario. There are obviously more complex situations in large accounts, but for the most part, you will typically see three levels of decision makers. Generally you have a C level, director level, and what I refer to as the front-line level. The front line is the contact in the trenches that deals with the daily grind of the company. These contacts get their hands dirty every day and are vital to the intricate workings of the company. The director level consists of those in middle management, and the C level includes upper management figures, such as VPs and "chief" officers like the CEO. When you lay these out, they resemble a staircase or hierarchy of decision makers.

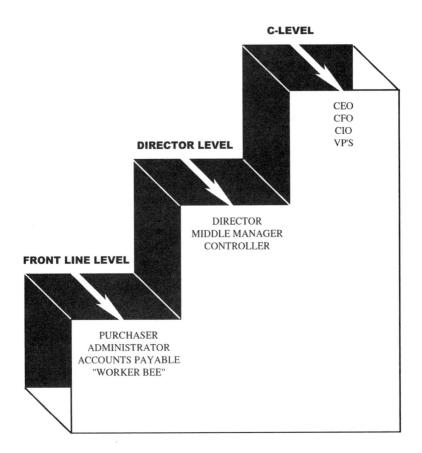

There is daily activity going on at each level. Within reason, each of these levels can somewhat act independently of the other. There may be buying decisions going on at the front-line level that are completely transparent to the C level. The C level may be planning on taking the company in an entirely different direction, unbeknownst to both the director and front-line levels. If we are not engaged in some fashion across each one of these areas, then we are limiting our knowledge and potential business within the account. Yes, there is something to be said for securing the relationships at the top C level, but if we only rely on that relationship, we are still limiting ourselves down the staircase.

It is critical that you have ongoing sales campaigns at each level of an organizational chart. Regardless of product, more times than not, it is beneficial to you that you have relationships up and down the staircase. Let's first look at a potential account-development plan for a net-new client, and then we will dive into some more basic concepts that can be applied to each level of the staircase.

For our scenario, we will be selling shoes to a major retailer. I have never sold shoes, nor do I really care to start, but for the purpose of this example, I simply want to show you that you can apply these concepts to most any situation.

The idea is pretty simple: we win over the account and have them buy our brand of shoes. So where do we start? As discussed in chapter two, activity is key. If we don't get in the game, then we seriously limit our chances of winning over the account. For our example, I specifically want to focus on how to use an organizational chart to complement your existing selling strategies. I am assuming that you would naturally be cold-calling your account and applying other standard sales techniques. I simply want to add to your already sound selling strategies.

If I were working this account, I would give myself the best chance of success by touching each level of the staircase at least three times with three different offerings. This would give me a total of nine unique touches across the entire company. With this being said, we have to realize that what is important to the C-level contact is most likely not important to the purchasing-level contact. Essentially, each level has its own specific needs. I would pinpoint those needs and develop a six-month campaign around three specific areas.

I would work each contact for five weeks with one campaign and then have a two-week preparation time to develop the next campaign. That means each campaign for each contact, including preparation, will last a total of seven weeks. Seven weeks multiplied by three campaigns is twenty-one weeks, which is pretty close to six months. So in summary, we have three contacts, three campaigns for each contact, across six months. A good way to remember this is 3+3=6.

Ideas for marketing to the C level need to be linked to increasing revenues and decreasing costs. Consider the following ideas:

- Importance of partnering with stable manufacturers
- What the competition has been doing with your brand
- How their company could break into a new market by taking on your line of shoes

Ideas for marketing to director level need to be focused on saving them time and reducing their headaches. Here are a few suggestions:

- Ease of implementation into the logistical environment
- Reduced touches with applicable product line
- Just-in-time inventory model

Ideas for marketing to the front-line level, or in this case, the purchasing level, need to be focused on saving them money and providing an easy ordering process. Try the following concepts:

- Online procurement system
- Easy/no-hassle return policy
- Free shipping on select products

Here is how a six-month campaign would break out for a C-level contact starting in January and ending in June:

- Jan. 2 to Jan. 13: Develop a direct mailer that focuses on the needs of applicable C-level contacts.
  - Drop it in the mail by Jan. 13 and allow one week for delivery.
  - Call to follow up in an effort to book an appointment over the next five weeks, Jan. 13 to Feb. 24.

- Feb. 27 to Mar. 10: Develop and mail the next marketing piece to send to C-level contacts.

  - Drop it in the mail by Mar. 10 and allow one week for delivery.

  - Mar. 17 to Apr. 21 follow up in an effort to book an appointment.

- Apr. 24 to May 5: Develop the next touch campaign to be sent to C-level contacts.

  - Drop it in the mail by May 5 and allow one week for delivery.

  - May 12 to June 16 follow up in an effort to book applicable appointment.

The important thing to keep in mind is that you would have two other campaigns going on at the exact same time at the director level and the purchasing level. Thus, at the end of six months, you will have touched three levels with three campaigns at each level. This gives you nine opportunities for them to say yes, spread across six months at three levels. That is quite a bit of exposure in an account. You can come up with whatever sort of campaign you like. I would use a direct-mail campaign for simplicity.

Assuming we can come up with a sales campaign for each level, we now need to look a little deeper into our target audience. At each level of the staircase, you will find selfish motives for these contacts. These are areas that fall outside our conventional selling concepts of saving time, money, and so on. Each of your contacts has personal and professional motivators. For example, you may be able to provide a just-in-time inventory for your director level contact, but it doesn't change the fact that he absolutely loathes the purchasing contact and can't stand to work with him or her. In a case like this, you would probably gain more buy-in with a solution that would limit the director level's interaction with the purchasing department. Or, on the other hand, you may be able to provide your purchasing contact the best online procurement system in the industry, but it doesn't change the fact that he or she is upset about being recently passed over for a promotion, and he or she is looking for a way to prove himself or herself to upper management. In an instance like this, you would want to strategically implement ideas that would make your purchasing contact look great in the eyes of management.

The above example referred to a net-new client. Keep in mind that it is important to have three levels of engagement with existing clients too. This is a little easier because you have already earned business within the account and have a sense of belonging. But don't forget; you want to have some form of a touch campaign going on at each level on a continual basis. This keeps you in front of the key players and will help you solidify the relationship across the account.

Your ideas for this campaign can be somewhat more personal since you are already in the account. Maybe if you want to get in front of the C level, you could thank them for the business and also refer to your working relationship with the people at the director level. As you see applicable material that you think would be of interest to them, you might simply drop it off at the front desk with a handwritten note. How you do it is up to you, but the important thing is to be dialed into each level of the organizational chart.

There are many variables that go into working an account. It is our responsibility as sales professionals to recognize our opportunities and develop a plan of action. I encourage you to look at what level you are spending your time on and explore other ways of branching out across an account. Too often I hear people say, "My guy is the main decision maker. I am fine just working with him." That may be true, but what happens when that person retires or leaves the company? Wouldn't it be nice to be spread across multiple contacts so that your income isn't solely resting on the shoulders of one person?

7

Partnering with Liaisons: Two Heads Are Better than One!

Have you ever heard the phrase "make your money work for you"? It basically means to invest your money and let it earn interest. The same concept can be used when it comes to partnering with liaisons or vendors. The relationships you invest in today will pay off down the road. In theory, you can "make your liaisons work for you." Wouldn't it be great to have a sales force of ten people closing deals and working accounts on your behalf? It isn't that hard to do. This chapter will look at various ways of getting people working for us without costing us any out-of-pocket expense.

As with anything associated with sales, we always need to be asking ourselves, "What's in it for me?" However, when we can decipher who, other than us, will benefit from a sale, we will see success much more quickly.

Take a simple residential home sale as an example: who benefits from the sale of a house? Perhaps some of the below listings could benefit from the sale of a house:

- Lending institution
- Local insurance company

- Title company
- Local lumberyard (repairs, remodeling, additions, etc)
- Local handyman
- Local lawn service

So if all these people are potential beneficiaries from the sale of a home, then doesn't it make sense to join forces and work together? If you can foster solid working relationships in these six areas, then don't you think they will recommend you as a listing agent whenever they hear of a home coming on the market? Of course they will! You probably wouldn't even need to give them a finder's fee because they would automatically see benefits from their relationship with you.

This concept can be applied to any form of sales. We always need to be looking at different ways of partnering with our liaisons. Sometimes you will run across selling solutions that allow you to actually go on joint sales calls with a partner. Anytime we can do joint sales calls or become involved with a product line that can fall into this category, we should embrace the opportunity. The technology industry is a perfect example of this concept.

In the technology industry, you have manufacturers, distributors, and resellers. The manufacturers sell to the distributors, the distributors sell to the resellers, and the resellers sell to the end user. The reason that there are so many hands touching the same product comes down to who owns the relationship. Manufacturers and distributors rely on the reseller to own the relationship with the client. Since the reseller owns the primary relationship with the client, the manufacturers are constantly hitting up the reseller to offer up their product first. The way they do this is by assigning manufacturer reps to the applicable reseller. This manufacturer rep will call on the reseller and communicate monthly offerings, ask how things are going, and so on and so forth. The other component is that, more times than not, you will find that manufacturers have field reps that are feet on the street. They are making customer calls and prospecting, just like everyone else. This means that if you work for a reseller, you can partner with a manufacturer rep, and you can also partner with the manufacturer's field reps. In theory, you could have the entire field-sales force of the manufacturer working with you.

Here is a theoretical example of how something like this would work:

Let's say we work for XYZ technology reseller, and we are based out of Milwaukee, Wisconsin. For the sake of this example, we are only authorized to sell products manufactured by ABC and DEF. Our product lines consist of servers, desktops, and laptops. We have a self-motivated interest to sell as much product as possible because this is obviously how we get paid. So, I have two manufacturers whose goods I can resell and three specific lines within each. Lastly, I am not limited by geographical constraints; I can resell product anywhere in the United States. What do I do?

I would align myself with both of these manufacturers and work as a team to increase sales and go on joint meetings. I would find out who the field reps were for both of these manufacturers, and I would foster positive working relationships with those field reps. Why? In the simplest terms, I want the field reps to throw business my way whenever they uncover an opportunity. If I am pushing their products, I want them to push my company as a viable sourcing option. If both of these companies have a combined sales force of twenty reps, that means I have twenty people working for me whenever they are on their sales calls or in other forms of meetings. Eventually, after the relationship is established, they will have me go on joint meetings with them, and I will do the same in return. We will work together as a team and have a unified front when meeting with customers.

This same concept can be used in any marketplace. Someone always benefits from a sale. Find out who benefits and partner with them. When you get a firm hold on this, your business will most likely explode.

It is important to be cognizant of your audience. It may be difficult to execute this idea if you haven't proven yourself to the potential partner. Perhaps it would be worthwhile to throw some unsolicited business their way before you approach them about the possibilities of a partnership. I would recommend that you put together a target list of viable partners, and then coordinate an applicable "attention" campaign. Once you have your list together and you have sent over some new business, then you have positioned yourself as someone who has earned the right to ask for time or a meeting. As long as the partners aren't competing directly against one another, you may even invite all them to an informal dinner where you can present your idea of working as a team or in a mutually beneficial way. The theory is simple: if we work together, we can grow our business. Before you know it, you will see a snowball effect to your teaming ideas, and business will be coming your way.

After you have a working list of partners, the next step is to coordinate client interaction. Cocktail hours and/or dinners are nice venues to introduce new contacts to one another. If you have four partners that you are working with (five including yourself), then I would recommend that each of you bring at least two net-new clients to the mixer. You now have a room of fifteen people with potential new business for everyone!

The point of these gatherings is to simply meet each other and exchange business cards. It doesn't have to be a formal selling presentation. Maybe you have a featured speaker for a general topic, but the real idea is to simply meet new contacts. When you meet someone new, make sure to jot down a note to yourself on the back of their business card. Use something simple, such as, "Met at dinner, John Smith introduced us." This way you can have information to break the ice when you call them in the following weeks.

Once you get the hang of partnering with liaisons and promoting yourself at events, then you will have an entirely new lead-generation program to work with. The best part is that these are warm leads. If you can do two or three events like this each month, you will start to see that the business comes easier, and the sales campaigns aren't as challenging.

A reliable beginning tactic at these events is to give a quick elevator pitch of what you do to the new contacts you meet. Since your message is basically the same at each event, you can now put mass follow-up packages together that can be mailed out to the people you met. Perhaps you include a handwritten note in each package referencing when and where you met the individual with a call to action for new business. Maybe you dedicate the last week of each month to sending out follow-up packages. If I were you, I would keep thirty or so packets available at all times. This will make it easier to mail them at the end of the month.

The goal is to execute on post-meeting follow-ups. You don't simply wait for new prospects to contact you; instead, you are proactive and contact them. The greatest part of this strategy is that these introductions were based solely off of working with people. You have used liaisons to get you in front of new contacts.

8

Time Management: Take Time to Make Time!

What would you do if you had an extra hour in the day to get your work done? Do you think you would be more productive? Have you tried to put together a time-management program but had difficulty sticking to it? I often hear people saying, "I just don't have the time to do it," or "There just aren't enough hours in the day." It is one of the oldest excuses in the book, but yet it is easy to overcome. The problem is that we usually don't want to take the time to make time. All we need to do is prioritize and plan accordingly.

Time management is a key element for almost any industry or profession. Everyone has critical tasks that need to be accomplished. The challenge is getting things accomplished in a timely fashion. So, how can we fit twelve hours of work into a ten-hour day? Prioritization and multitasking are the answers.

The biggest reason people can't get their work done is due to the fact that they lose focus and are easily taken off track. We may have the best intentions of prospecting ten new customers, but the minute we get into the office, we are hit with a disaster that takes away our prospecting time. I am sure that everyone can relate to these types of situations. It comes up everyday. In order to overcome these unexpected hurdles, we need to have a plan in place. We also need to stick to the plan and not waiver.

In my industry, prospecting was my lifeline. If I stopped prospecting for new business, I would eventually fail. Needless to say, I figured out a way to fit it into my schedule. Here are the critical areas that I had to cover each day in order to be successful:

- Cold-call at least ten net new prospect accounts
- Expand product lines into existing accounts
- Follow up on quotes/orders
- Handle unexpected issues with orders
- Return voice mails and e-mails

I could expand this list, but these five areas are sufficient for our example. On the surface, it doesn't seem all that difficult.

The biggest killer of my day was the unexpected emergency issues or needs. It seemed that the more successful I became, the more difficult it was to manage my time. When I was a rookie, it was a breeze. I only had a handful of customers, so it wasn't like I was being stretched to the max. Once I had become more successful and grown my business, I quickly realized that I was going to have to figure out a way to get my five areas completed but also take care of the unexpected fires. Figuring out the plan was the most difficult part. Executing it was fairly easy.

I knew that the most important part of my day was cold-calling new accounts. I had to figure out what was preventing me from doing this. Think about it: if I was neglecting the most important part of my day, I was cheating myself. Remember: sales is a self-centered game. If I didn't have new customers, I would not succeed. I had to make it my top priority to always be prospecting for new business. Coupled with this, I had to make sure my existing customers didn't feel neglected.

What I did may have been antiquated, but it worked nonetheless. I kept a running journal of what events happened during my day for one week. I started each day with the best intentions of making ten new prospect calls (which took about an hour or so). I quickly found that I would only make it through two or three calls before I got distracted with something else. Typically, it was an "urgent" request for a quote or something similar. What I figured out at the end of my week may be something comparable to your current obstacles. E-mail and incoming calls were totally consuming my time. I had to develop a strategy that would allow me to be back in control of my day. Here is what I did: I prioritized my day, and I used my calendar to help me stay on track.

I always felt that mornings were the best time to cold-call, so I scheduled all of my cold calls to take place from 8:00 AM until 9:00 AM. The key component was that I didn't check e-mail, voice mail, or answer incoming calls during this time. As a matter of fact, for the first few weeks, I didn't even open my e-mail until I had completed the cold calls. I would answer voice mails and return e-mails between 9:00 AM and 10:00 AM. Then I would call to expand new product lines between the hours of 10:00 AM and 12:00 PM. I was able to hit my most critical areas before 12:00 PM. I used the last part of my day to call existing customers, enter quotes, mail letters, and the like.

The catalyst to successful time management was the ability to multitask while I was progressing through my day. I always was looking at ways to get the most out of each phone call or meeting. If I knew I had to call a customer back to discuss a quote, I would also bring up a new product category with him or her while we were on the phone. This put me back in charge of my day.

I *really* liked it when customers would call me. Why? Because I knew if they had time to pick up the phone and call me, then they had time to talk! I would always get the most out of my incoming call because I knew they had available time to talk or they wouldn't have called me. I would hit them up for referrals, for new product categories, for more quotes, to set up a meeting, and so on. It was a great way to multitask and accomplish my daily goals.

I did the same thing in e-mails. If a customer wanted me to give him or her tracking information for a product, I would always add an additional line asking him or her about an upcoming project or a chance to quote a new product. My e-mail would read, "Mr. Customer, your package is en route and should be delivered by 10:30 AM. Your tracking number is 12345678910. By the way, do you have a few minutes this week to discuss your XYZ needs? I have a couple ideas in mind that I think would benefit your company."

You've heard of killing two birds with one stone? I was knocking the entire flock out of the air. The most important thing is that I did it with professionalism. When you are rocking and rolling through your day, your customers can sense it. They can feel your energy.

If you are a road warrior, the same system applies. Most likely you have to check your e-mail and voice mail before you leave your house. In the grand scheme of things, it just comes down to blocking off specific times to do your main tasks during the day. Don't sell yourself short by neglecting the things that will make you successful. Keep a file folder with you of all your prospects and their phone numbers. Take time out of your day to make the calls and do what is necessary.

Utilizing technology is another way of staying on task and optimizing time management. If you find yourself traveling on a regular basis, then it may be wise to invest in a mobile device to check your e-mail and voice mail while traveling. I heard of one example of a real estate agent in the Chicago area who was struggling with getting all of his business done in a timely fashion. Because he was out of the office most of the time, his service levels were slipping, and it was taking him too long to return calls. He purchased a mobile device and quickly became the number one agent at his branch.

Another way to use technology as a time management tool may be to invest in a viable contact-manager program. Not only will this allow you to organize all of your client/prospect information, but it will also allow you to quickly use this information to your advantage. If you come across a fantastic offering, you can use your contact-manager tool to send a mass e-mail to your client list communicating the offering. There are programs that will auto-populate the e-mail with your clients' first names in order to give a more personal feel. Not only can you send e-mails, but you can also send voice mails. In theory, you can individually touch hundreds of clients with a voice mail and/or an e-mail within seconds. Use your best judgment depending on the situation and your client base.

Once you have accomplished a solid selling foundation and have started generating a respectable revenue stream, you may want to bring on an assistant. This doesn't necessarily have to be someone that you put on the payroll (although it could be if you wanted). Instead, you could join forces with a newer salesperson and possibly work with them to off-load some of your accounts or split new accounts. This will put money in his or her pocket and free your time to ultimately do what you do best—sell. Maybe you work out a fifty-fifty split for accounts you send that salesperson's way, as long as he or she does all the administrative work. Only you will know what your true balance is with these sorts of pairings. If your current accounts are hindering you from getting new business, then maybe it is a smart move. What you give up today may pay off hugely in the long run. Again, the ultimate decision has to be yours.

It is important to truly manage your business. By managing your business, you can tell where you have gaps and what you need to do in order to make it to the next level. A teaming approach may be just the thing you need to get to the next step. If your efforts have worked thus far to point X, then you may have hit your maximum capacity. It is possible that you will only be able to grow your business by a small amount unless you partner with someone. An easy way to see where you are with your book of business is to look at your peers' books. If your peers are doing significantly better than you without assistants, then maybe you don't need one just yet. Or maybe you are one of the top performers. Take a look at your numbers and see if there has been any significant growth over the last six months. If not, then maybe it's time to bring on an assistant. Whatever you do, make sure that you are focused on sales activity.

Don't bring on an assistant to sell for you. An assistant should be used to set up appointments, do administrative work, and so on. The sales side of the business should fall on your shoulders most of the time. The exception would be if it is low-level stuff that doesn't really need your attention. You can use the low-level activity as a training ground for your assistant and then gradually give them more responsibility. At the end of the day, when it comes down to success or failure, make sure you are the one in charge of the sales process.

One of the most overlooked areas in time management is to simply "do it right the first time." If we could conduct our day without having to touch the same issue or topic multiple times, then we would greatly increase our efficiency. This is an area that can only be evaluated on a personal level from your part. In my industry, one of the time killers is dealing with RMAs (Returns). If I could reduce my RMAs to zero, then I could focus more of my efforts on sales as opposed to administrative tasks. One thing I do to prevent RMAs is to have another set of eyes look over the order before I send it out. This two-minute double check will hopefully prevent a return that will take up a significant amount of time. For certain products, there is a no-return policy that comes directly from the manufacturer. For these types of products, I have the client send me an e-mail of acknowledgment that he or she has reviewed the quote and the specifications meet his or her needs. This covers both parties, and it has caught several potential RMAs over the years.

If there are areas of your business that are simply too time consuming and drag down your day, I encourage you to be proactive and formulate a small task force to come up with a more streamlined approach. If you gather a few of the top performers together and use a professional approach to the problem, you should be able to come up with some viable solutions. Upper management should welcome your recommendations. If you can't get management's interest, then use your available resources to address the problem on your own individual level.

A more rudimentary idea may simply be to make a handwritten list of your to-do's. Prioritize the list according to you particular needs, and simply execute the to-do's. The important thing to remember is to only keep one list. If you have more than one, you will most likely forget about one of them. Keep one list and simply review your to-do's at the beginning of the day and at the end of the day. This will force you to keep the list up to date at the beginning of each day with the things you need to do and also hold yourself accountable at the end of the day to check your progress.

These concepts can be applied across any industry or profession. All you have to do is prioritize and execute. Figure out what the key success factors are and then address them accordingly. Time management isn't that difficult if you simply take the time to make time. You may have to spend a few weeks figuring out the proper course of action, but as long as you have a solid plan and execute the plan, you should be okay. If you continue to be reactive as opposed to proactive, you will fail more times than not. Be proactive in your approach, and you will take control of your day.

9

Listening: There Is a Reason We Have Two Ears and One Mouth

If you've ever had the chance to experience a meeting where a team member didn't know when to shut up, it is probably very painful to recall the experience. If you haven't yet experienced the headstrong sales approach, then think of running one's fingernails down a chalkboard, or possibly drinking a glass of grapefruit juice while eating chocolate cake. Both scenarios will give you a good summation of the experience.

For some reason, there is an assumption that to be a good sales rep, one needs to constantly be talking and pushing his or her product. In short, some people feel that, "If I give the customer a chance to talk, I lose control of the process. I'm the expert, and I know more than my customer." I have been around plenty of top-level executives who needed to "be seen and not heard." I have even been in meetings where my own CEOs and VPs would ask me why I wasn't contributing to the conversation. To be perfectly honest, I never saw any reason to fill the air with meaningless chitchat that would have been forgotten within thirty seconds. There are times when I was almost tempted to ask the client if they were really listening or even cared what had just been said.

How can one possibly know what to tell a client if one hasn't taken the time to actually listen to the client? Why is it that people assume they automatically know what people need or want to hear? If you can hear yourself talking, then be quiet and do more listening.

Yes, there are exceptions to every rule, but in general, listen more and talk less. You would be surprised at the amount of information that can be picked up just by shutting your mouth and listening. A lot of times, people are so concerned about what they want to say that they don't even hear the vital information that may help them close a deal or solidify a relationship. People think that they need to impress a client with their vast knowledge of XYZ subject matter when that usually isn't the case.

Hey, I have been to plenty of dinners where the best part of the experience was the steak, potatoes, check, and maybe a nice Clos du Bois cabernet thrown in for good measure. I would have been much more content eating by myself in the bar than listening to the meaningless banter at the table. Who really cares? Don't waste my time, and don't think people really care about what you're talking about just because they are smiling. What they are really thinking is, "I couldn't be any less interested in what this person is saying than I am at this very minute. I wonder what I am going to have for dessert. I think I will go with the cheesecake."

I was at a dinner party one time when a guy talked for at least fifteen minutes about the process of catching a lobster and preparing it for dinner, and how cruel it was. The entire time I was trying to figure out how to fake a food allergy so that I could exit stage left. I finally asked the guy if lobsters could count. He looked at me as if I was from Mars. So I asked again, "Have you ever seen a lobster that could count to three?" He said, "Well, no." I responded, "Until lobsters can count; they will remain at the top of the list as my favorite seafood. Please pass the butter."

My point is this: It is okay to have normal conversations, but you don't have to be doing all the talking all of the time. Don't be afraid to turn loose of the reins. You don't need to talk for fifteen minutes about something that doesn't matter to simply fill dead air.

So how can we be seen and not heard and still achieve success? The last thing we want to do is come across as a stick in the mud. Or even worse, we don't want to seem aloof or arrogant. So how can we politely engage in conversation but still establish credibility? The key is this: since most people like to talk, our job is rather easy. We simply need to let the clients tell us about their needs and what they feel is important. We may need to ask some clarifying questions once in a while, but for the most part we really need to let the clients do most of the talking so that we can figure out where we may be able to help them. If we do the majority of the talking, we don't give the clients ample opportunity to communicate their pain points or concerns.

Let's just assume for the moment that our product/offering is above board and a quality product. In order to properly win over our clients, we need to know where they need help. The best way to get this information is to listen. If the conversation comes to a grinding halt, of course it's okay to throw out a curveball about something off the cuff. But, it is important to get the ball back in their court and get them talking. Try a simple conversation starter, such as, "John, you mentioned earlier that you have fifteen distribution centers. I can only imagine the organization required to manage something of that magnitude. Tell me more about how you do it." It would take me all of ten seconds to prompt the client, and then I shut up and listen. At the end of the conversation, the client will probably be so taken off guard that someone actually listened to what he or she had to say that he or she may even give you the business based on that alone.

The next thing to keep in mind is that most, although not all, of the time, we have the benefit of being able to have more than one engagement with the prospect. I have seen too many instances where a sales rep feels this is their one and only shot to "wow" the client. In doing so, the sales rep overwhelms the potential prospect and ruins any chance of a follow-up meeting. Be patient and listen. Live to fight another day. Gather your information and present it at a later time.

Use an introduction that is not overbearing, such as, "John, we have been corresponding for about two months now, and I think I may have an offering that will help you. Would you have a couple hours to talk next week?" Now you're on! Now you talk! You have days, weeks, even months of information that you have been filling away. You are prepared and informed. You now know where the true problems are, where your competition is weak, and how to win the battle.

I can't tell you how many times I have been in a meeting and the customer said something like, "I just wish I had someone that could drop ship to remote locations." I would quickly glance at the sales rep, and I could tell he or she was about to come out of his or her seat with a frontal assault of "We can do that! That is our specialty! No one does it better than us!" I would give them a gesture of "easy partner; I know what you're thinking but just relax and don't say anything." More times than not, the customer would come up with something else that he or she needed.

If I had let the rep loose like a bull in a china shop, the client would have been so overwhelmed and focused on drop shipping that he or she wouldn't have mentioned he or she also needed ABC and XYZ. Write it down, make a mental note, and continue to let the client talk. Even go to the point where you simply say, "John, thank you for taking the time to meet with me today. If it's okay with you, I am going to take my notes back to the office and think about some areas where we can help you. Maybe we could get together in a couple weeks to discuss potential offerings. In the mean time, is it okay to call or e-mail you if I have other questions?"

What you are doing is laying the foundation for additional correspondence so that you can have time to think about the best solution. More than likely you have enough information from the first meeting that you already know if you have a better solution. However, there is no perceived value in such a quick proposal, plus the client may come up with other areas that you may be able to help with. Things like this should take time. It helps you to prove yourself and establish your credibility. You get to meet with the customer numerous times to develop a personable relationship. This way when you say, "John, you know, if you are serious about XYZ, I think I have a viable solution," he will actually take you seriously.

Don't be afraid to turn the conversation over to the client. Your job is to be a meeting facilitator and simply absorb the information. The more listening you do, the better off you will be. If you find yourself constantly jumping into the conversation, force yourself to take more notes. This will not only make you stay quiet, but it will show the client that you are taking him or her seriously. Keep a list of "prompting" questions with you in case the conversation comes to a standstill.

It is also important to be cognizant of doing your part to keep a good balance with the client; the relationship is important. Keep equilibrium in the conversation between your agenda and the client's personal interests. It is perfectly acceptable to talk about current events or sports at length if that is where the client wants to go. Eventually you will get to the point where your business conversation is about five minutes and your non-business conversation is about fifty-five minutes. This is when your career truly becomes fun!

Not only is listening key in a face-to-face selling environment, but it also plays a huge part when it comes to phone calls. A few years ago, I was working a high-profile account that had done very little business with me, comparatively speaking. I was working the VP of Operations pretty heavily, but I couldn't seem to get the lion's share of the business. I managed to get some business but nothing much, just breadcrumbs for the most part.

The only area in which I was really making any progress was gathering information. I had been working the account for several months, and I always seemed to be able to carry on decent conversations with the main players. Keep in mind this was all done over the phone. I would call to thank them for the business, and we would chat about football and whatnot. Over these discussions, I would simply prompt the conversation and then sit back and let them talk. I was building a case with this information so that I could present it at a later time. They would tell me their pain points, and I would listen. They would also tell me personal information about themselves as well. For example, I found out that the VP was a huge New York Giants football fan. Rather than jump at the first chance I saw, I instead filed this information away for a later day. This would give me ample time to prepare and hopefully sound intelligent when I presented my solution.

The VP felt comfortable with me, and we built a rapport over the phone for several months. I took all of my information, and when I felt the time was right, I used it. I invited the VP to Chicago for a Bears v. Giants football game so that we could discuss his account in greater detail. He accepted, and before I knew it, I was sitting next to a contact I had never met but had spoken to over the phone for almost a year. I had built the relationship entirely over the phone and earned his trust simply by listening and taking care of his account. If I had immediately invited him out for a Bears-Giants game I doubt he would have accepted. I needed to listen and build rapport.

Long story short, this ended up being a multimillion-dollar account. Had I not been listening, I would have simply been another sales rep that was trying to steamroll my way into the business. Had I not been calculated in my process, I would have seemed too eager and possibly pushed him away.

The lesson is to listen more and talk less.

10

Executing on Basic Principles: Imitation Is the Best Form of Flattery!

Up to this point, we have touched upon nine key elements that will help us turn into a Super Sales Rep. What do we do with all of this newfound knowledge? We put it into action. I would suggest taking baby steps until you can knock out a detailed thirty-, sixty-, and ninety-day plan of attack. The idea is to take the concepts in these chapters and tailor them to your own style and methods. However, before we go off and start cold-calling CEOs, we still need to be aware of our surroundings and look at ways to expand on the ideas already discussed in this book. If we can blend the preceding ideas with what has been working for others, then we only increase our success level. The next few paragraphs will discuss different ways of executing these basic principles coupled with best practices.

What are the top performers doing? I would take a look at what they have been doing and evaluate if it makes sense for your specific goals. Maybe you can use some of their strategies in your daily approach. You may be able to talk one of them into being your mentor. The idea is to see what has been working for them and somehow use it to complement your own style. Try offering to take them to lunch once a month to discuss different ideas. If you are fortunate enough to get the ear of a top performer, ask how his or her approach would be different. If he or she had it to do over again, what are the changes he or she would have made? What wouldn't he or she do? What were the things that were a hindrance as opposed to being helpful? What would he or she do more of and less of?

In addition to top performers, I would look at your competitors. They may be blowing the doors off the market by having some sort of new concept in their sales approach. Don't be afraid to press your customers on what your competition has been doing. Also, you may be able to leverage some of your liaisons to get you the inside scoop on your competition. Pick and chose what works best for your applicable product lines.

Police yourself on a regular basis. If you are truly motivated and honestly want to be successful, then you can keep an ongoing tally of your performance. I would put forth the due diligence to develop a working schedule and stick to it the best you can. Start out making a five-day schedule, and then develop it into a thirty-day calendar. The important thing is to maximize productivity within your day. You are the only one that knows if you have been putting forth maximum effort. Don't cheat yourself out of success. The sales game is hard enough by itself; there is no need to be your own worst enemy. Prioritize and execute.

In addition to a legitimate schedule, you would also want to incorporate some industry routines into your career. If you see that top performers are taking clients to dinner, then you need to figure out a way to do it as well. Perhaps you should look at allocating one day a week to dining out with a client. Also, it may be helpful to obtain industry certifications. This will not only give you more credibility, but it may allow you an opportunity to interact with other people in your industry from other companies. Another idea is to look at the activities that the successful people do outside of work. Maybe they read sales books or attend industry seminars. Reflect on what they're doing that you are not doing. The goal of these steps is to prompt you to find different ways of bettering yourself.

Have you heard the expression "If you hang around millionaires you will be a millionaire. If you hang around bums you will be a bum"? It basically means you are a product of your environment and your actions. Look to see if you can find common themes in the lifestyles of successful people. This is a bit of a stretch, but it can be done with a little effort. For example, gather information on their daily routines, and try to imitate the areas that are achievable. You can find a lot of information on the Internet from interviews with notable, talented people. You may find a common thread that some of these people start their day at 5:00 AM and begin with exercise in the morning. Who knows what you will find? The important thing is to dig deep to understand their idiosyncrasies that you can apply to your own life. There may be some truth to the old saying "early to bed, early to rise makes a man healthy, wealthy, and wise." Or, stay out all night and party like a rock star; the choice is entirely yours.

In addition to the aforementioned steps, you may also want to investigate what is happening in other industries. If you are in healthcare, you may want to check out what the sales folks are doing in the textile business. You don't know what you don't know. Don't be afraid to think outside the box. Call a non-competing or non-industry vendor and ask them to lunch to discuss ideas. Taking a completely different approach to your sales strategy may be what you have been missing. People from other industries could help you come up with unique ideas.

Maybe the easiest thing to do is simply evaluate what has been working for you and what hasn't been working for you. If you have seen success with a certain market segment or product line, then focus more of your efforts in those particular areas. Before you start a new sales campaign, stop to think about what your existing clients have been purchasing. Take these trends and use them to your advantage when working other accounts or prospects. Is there a time during the day when you feel better than other times? If so, utilize this for your most important tasks. Look back at your successful months and dissect what made them successful. Recognize these factors and work to duplicate them in your upcoming months.

Look at what low performers have been doing, and don't do it! You would be surprised by what you can learn from someone that is failing. It sounds harsh, but if it helps you in your own personal development, then that's the breaks. Take time to stop and listen to the low performers on the phone. Listen to how they run their sales calls and ask yourself what you would do differently. Take a look at their outward appearance. Do they look successful, or do they look like they are failing miserably? How is their professionalism and preparation? Are they proactive with their business or reactive? Make sure to take a mental note of the things that jump out at you and address them accordingly.

There are many different ways of investing in yourself. The important thing is to continually be raising the bar. If you get comfortable, you will fall. Sales isn't an area that you can approach at 80 percent-commitment levels. You have to max out your commitment each and every month. If you think you have all the answers, you are wrong. Use best-practice sharing and proven methodologies for bettering yourself. Don't be afraid to ask for help. Asking for help isn't a sign of weakness. Asking for help is actually a sign that someone is intelligent enough to realize he or she needs coaching and development. It shows that he or she takes his or her career seriously. Look outside conventional thinking, and you may be surprised by what you will find.

11

Dos and Don'ts of the Daily Grind: Ride the Wave and Never Complain!

Whenever I am having a great day, I always push myself to engage with customers. I believe that success and momentum are contagious. There may be an entire month when I am really in the groove. We have all had those months. Everything seems to be coming together, and we are really putting some very solid things on the table. That is the time to step it up and push yourself even harder.

Too often, people will have a great accomplishment and then bask in the glory of their most recent victory. The reality is that this is the perfect time to become proactive and put it into overdrive. People call it luck, coincidence, or a number of things, but I think that clients can feel our success, and we can use all of this positive energy to our advantage. When good things are happening to us, common sense tells us that we are just more pleasant to be around. We have a little hop to our step; we have a little more gleam to our smile; we have a pleasant tone. Customers want to do business with successful people.

When you are feeling positive and doing well, get on the phone and get in front of the customers! Don't be afraid to tell them how things are going and how excited you are about the month. Encourage them to comment as well:

"Mr. Customer, things are just going crazy right now; there is so much new business coming in it is like prospecting for gold. I bet it's the same for you too, right? What's happening on your end? Are they keeping you busy?"

Who in their right mind will tell you, "No, it's really slow right now, and come to think of it, I don't even know why they keep me on the payroll."

More than likely, you will get a mirrored response of what you emit. Customers are eager to share in the excitement. They might say, "You know, it is really crazy over here too! We just bought a new plant and I am working twelve hours a day just trying to keep up!"

Strike while the iron is hot. Communicate your success and engage the customer to participate as well. Once the bridge has been established, immediately dive in for new opportunities. Use a positive and helpful approach, such as, "You guys are bringing on a new plant? Why didn't you tell me? I would love to have a chance to help you guys with that project. How can I get in the loop?" Remember to always capitalize on the power of your success and continue the momentum.

Conversely, no one likes a whiner. The important thing to remember is that you are ultimately responsible for your own success. A true champion will suck it up and figure out a way to make it work. A loser will immediately look for someone to blame. I have seen it time and time again. The top performers may have a bad month or an issue with an order. Rarely will they ever blame someone else, even if it truly was someone else's fault. Most often you will hear them say: "Let's figure out how to learn from this and move on." On the flip side, when people with a negative attitude have an issue, everyone in the office will hear about it. Why? They do this because they want to blame someone else for their own failures. Misery loves company. If you don't believe me, just look at how many successful people stick around the water cooler when someone starts complaining. Rarely will you see a successful person jump on the bandwagon of pointing fingers. However, successful people will get caught up in a wave of positive energy.

I have been in sales meetings where negative people stuck out like a sore thumb. It is almost comical. One particular incident comes to mind. We were recognizing top performers for a job well done, and everyone was congratulating them and wishing them continued success. I looked over at this certain individual who I will call the Lemon Drop (it looks good on the outside, but it is sour in reality), and the look on his face was almost one of disgust. It was all I could do to keep from laughing. This type of behavior would frustrate most managers, but to me it was amusing. I find it funny that someone was so bitter with his own shortcomings that he couldn't be happy for a peer who was doing well. Jealousy and bitterness, oh the tangled web we weave.

Rather than offer up congratulations, this person simply sat in his chair and said nothing. After the initial congratulatory portion was over, I opened the discussion up to the group for questions and interaction. I am a big believer in best-practice sharing, and I feel that others can benefit from trading ideas within the group. So let's set the stage quickly: we have just congratulated the top performers for a job well done and have now opened up a Q&A session for everyone to ask these top reps how they do what they do. The mood is light and happy, and everyone is smiling, except for our lone Lemon Drop.

During the course of the Q&A, there were some really good ideas flying around. I was very impressed by the quality of the discussion. People were writing down ideas, and you could feel the energy level building. It was great. We were really getting somewhere, and it was fantastic. Thus far, there was still nothing from our Lemon Drop. He was being quiet, and that was perfectly fine with me. Then the tide turned. Someone posed a question from the group, and it was as if everything went into to slow motion. It was like a dream where everything slows down and you know something bad is about to happen. This particular question happened to be a sore spot for our Lemon

Drop, and before I could head it off at the pass, our Lemon Drop was throwing a tantrum.

He went on a rant that lasted for a good forty-five seconds without taking a breath. I didn't have a chance to throw out any countermeasures or divert the certain catastrophe. The group and I were like a bunch of sitting ducks, and Lemon Drop was picking us off one at a time. The forty-five seconds of negative energy totally changed the entire meeting. You could see the looks on people's faces; they were very disappointed. Luckily for us, the true champions of the group simply ignored the negative energy and went on about their business. However, the collateral damage had been done, and we cut our meeting short. Lemon Drop was miserable, and he wanted everyone else to be miserable with him. He ruined a great meeting.

Don't be a lemon drop! No one likes to be around a lemon drop. Be positive and upbeat. Fight through the hard times and lift yourself up to be a better person. Don't take the easy way out and complain about shortcomings that are out of your control. It only makes you look negative and will turn people off. Take ownership of your success by looking in the mirror and understanding that you and you alone are responsible for your future.

How many times do you see a professional sports coach complain about poor officiating as the reason they lost the game? Rarely will this ever happen. I have seen many games where an umpire may have missed a critical call, and ultimately it resulted in a loss for the affected team. During a post-game press conference, one would almost expect the coach to take the easy way out and blame the officiating for the loss. However, more times than not, the coach will hold his head up high and take responsibility for the loss as opposed to passing blame onto someone else. A true champion doesn't look for a scapegoat on which to pin his or her downfall. Instead, he or she takes responsibility and shoulders the burden. Quite often you will hear the coach say something to the tune of, "Well, the score shouldn't have been that close in the first place. It is our own fault for letting the game get so close that it hinged on one call." Could this apply to your situation? Have you ever missed a sales goal because an order didn't make it out on time? If one order kept you from hitting your goal, then perhaps you could have sold a little more to keep it from happening? On the other hand, you could look at the glass as half full and view it as a great start to the next month.

Successful people don't complain; they overcome.

12

Tricks of the Trade: How Do They Do That?

Have you ever wondered how to get past the gatekeeper when contacting a potential client? How about how to increase your margins and not lose a customer? There are times when we find ourselves wrapped up in an account that is either not giving us the time of day or possibly being very difficult to work with. For the most part, clients generally are respectful of your career and understand your intentions. However, from time to time you will run across a problematic account that expects you to work for free and couldn't care less about how you may be able to help it. Or, you may find accounts that simply don't want to talk to you at all. Sometimes the answers to these challenging situations only come with experience; other times solutions are a little easier to find. Here are some common challenges with some plausible solutions. Feel free to pick and choose from the below list and use them when and where you want:

1. How can I get around the gatekeeper?

   a. Call before or after normal working hours. This increases the likelihood that the gatekeeper is not in the office. If you are calling the right contacts, most likely they start early and finish late. You will have a better chance of getting them late at night when everyone is out of the office.

b. Take the gatekeeper out of the equation. You will frequently find that decision makers are more apt to pick up an internal call as opposed to one coming in from the outside. You can call into a different division within the company and have them transfer you over to the person you want to speak with. For example, you can call into Accounting or HR and have them transfer you over to the direct line of the person you actually wanted to speak with. More times than not, they will send you directly through as opposed to sending you over to the administrative assistant. The call will come through from an internal extension, instead of appearing as though it came in from the outside.

c. Ask the gatekeeper what you have to do in order to get through. This is a simple yet powerful idea—actually putting your cards on the table and asking them.

2. How can I increase margins?

a. Secure the sale first; worry about margin second. Increasing margins is somewhat of an art. The important thing to keep in mind is that you need to secure the sale at a "fair" margin for both parties. Once you have secured the sale, you may be able to work with your suppliers and others to lower your actual costs.

b. Find out the levels of the customer's buying power. For example, let's say your customer has a company credit card, and he or she has the authority to purchase anything up to five thousand dollars. Most likely you can guess that if they are talking to you about a purchase that is under five thousand dollars, you are not up against any competition. Here is how you do it: "Mr.

Customer, we have two hundred of those units in stock, so delivery shouldn't be an issue. How many are you looking for?" (Customer will respond) "Okay, I can put the order in today and have them to you in about a week." The response of the customer should dictate your next move. If he or she says, "Okay, place the order," then you can charge anything you want within reason. If they say, "What is my price?" then you need to say, "They are around $X a piece, and your total order should come in right around $XXX." If they are okay with this, then you just made yourself a few extra margin points. If they push you again and say something like, "I need an exact price," then don't fight them. You should respond by saying, "No problem, I will put together a quote and send it over ASAP with exact numbers. How soon are you looking to make the purchase? Is this something you can move forward on today, or do you have to wait for everyone to get back to you with competitive quotes?" You have now given yourself three shots of raising your margins.

c. Secure the sale and offer an alternative product after you have won the deal. Let's say you are quoting against three major competitors, and price is the only driving factor. You obviously have to come in at a low margin to win the deal. However, the real "selling" starts after you have secured the purchase order. This is where you call the *end users* of the product (the people that will actually be using the product) and thank them for their business and let them know you are excited to be working with them. The idea is that you are looking for ways to add to your order and/or change the components of the order. For example, let's say you just secured a large deal for cardboard boxes. You would call the people in the warehouse and let them know you will be working with them. During the course of conversation, let them know that you can also ship those cardboard boxes with a pre-printed company logo. More than likely the end user doesn't care about price, and they will want the logo to be on the box. You simply use them as a champion so that you can add on an extra line item to your already secured order. You most likely won't have to re-quote this add-on product.

d.   Depending on the industry you are in, overnight or expedited delivery can be a key sign for high margins. If a customer is asking you things such as, "Can you can get it to me tomorrow?" or "How soon can you get this to me? I need it right away," this means that he or she needs it fast. Most likely the contact forgot to order something, or he or she is going to look very foolish if XYZ unit doesn't show up by tomorrow morning. If you have a situation like this, then you need to kick it into high gear and secure the order immediately with a heightened sense of urgency. You can respond, "Mr. Customer, it looks like I have the units in stock, but we need to move on these right away. It's going to be about $X before tax. I will mark it as high priority and expedite the order. What purchase order number would you like me to use?" Once the client give you the PO number, you can basically charge anything you want as long as it is close to the approximate number you gave him or her. You are providing a service. Clients should be okay paying a premium dollar amount for your professional execution and delivery. Buying with confidence comes with a price tag. This is why you always want to earn their business and continue to prove yourself. They will never question you when they are really in a jam.

3. They meet with me, but they won't buy from me.

   a. This is just the tip of the iceberg. More than likely, the real issue is commitment. Your customer is doing a lot of talking but not committing to you. The best thing to do is start small and move forward in baby steps. Here are a few ways of securing commitment: Secure a signed credit application. Have the customer come to your office for a meeting and/or company tour. Have the customer attend an off-site seminar or trade show with you so that you can discuss upcoming rollouts and such. Inform the customer that you will be bringing your boss and/or VP with you on the next meeting. This will allow you to respectfully push your customer on his or her intentions.

   b. Get tickets to a sporting event or perhaps a luncheon. Make it a stipulation that you would like to invite the customer and his or her boss.

   c. Tell the customer that you are bringing your boss with you on the next meeting, and you would like it if he or she arranged to have his or her boss there as well.

4. My contact won't let me go over his or her head to other contacts.

   a. If the account isn't buying from you, who cares? Do it anyway; you have nothing to lose.

   b. Go over the contact's head with the intention of thanking the higher-ups for their business, checking their view of your customer service, and also to tell them how great of a job your day-to-day contact is doing. It doesn't matter if they are buying from you or not. You can always call the main person in charge and simply say, "John and I have some really good things in the works. I really enjoy working with him; what other projects do you have on the books for this year?"

5. My account always shops me on price and needs three competitive quotes.

    a. Give your customer the quotes but include another offering as well. If he or she is asking for a quote for XYZ, then also include a comparable offering for ABC. This will allow you to change the field of competition and be the only one quoting your amended version.

    b. Ask these types of accounts about their criteria for quoting. Most people will say price. Tell them that you will always give them the lowest price, but you need to be the last one to quote. Let them know you will give them your raw cost on the product, and they can mark it up to whatever they feel is fair. This will allow them to get the lowest price, and you can also make a little money. This is a difficult argument for your customers to overcome. If they really want the lowest price, then you just gave them the keys to the kingdom. If they fight you on this, then go over their heads and let their boss know that you are doing everything in your power to help them secure low pricing, but you and your daily contact may be misunderstanding each other. Once the boss gets word that you are willing to give them your raw cost, you will get their attention. Eventually you will become the vendor of choice, and all of these issues will go away. Your main goal is to become the partner of choice; sometimes you have to dance a little in order to make it happen.

    c. Depending on the time frame of the project, you may be able to play a little of the futures game in your industry. You will often find that companies are securing large quotes today for something that will be closing in six months. For argument's sake, you can quote them anything you want today because when they do get around to making the purchase, your initial quote will need to be revised and the products may be obsolete. So, depending on the industry, make sure you qualify the time frame of the purchase and then simply lowball the initial quote. You are banking on price drops and/or changes in the needs of the customer, and so on. If you have several months of planning, this should be pretty easy to position in your favor. You will blow the competition away in your initial quote, and they may not even get a chance to re-quote. Also, you may impress the customer so much that they will give you some incremental orders in the mean time.

6. They won't return my calls.

   a. Have you given these accounts a reason to call you back? Offer up tickets to an event or sporting activity. It doesn't even matter if there is an event or not. You can say, "Mr. Customer, we are putting together a potential invite list for the upcoming game between the Bears and Packers. If there is enough customer interest, it should be a good time. Is this something you would be interested in?" You're not lying. There are so many vendors out there that want to partner with you; it shouldn't be that hard to put something like this together.

   b. Let these contacts know that you are getting internal pressure to either close their account or keep it open. You really need them to call you back so that you can tie up these loose ends of either closing their credit limits or keeping them open.

   c. After all else fails, you can leave them a voice mail that starts out saying, "John, I am going to be calling your CEO tomorrow, and I just wanted to keep you in the loop. If you have any questions, feel free to call me at 555-1212." You have to get that on their voice mail immediately. If you wait too long, they will just delete your message. Make sure you immediately start out saying, "John, I am going to be calling XYZ contact tomorrow." Then you can say who you are, what the purpose of the call is, and any other relevant information.

7. I can't expand my product offering.

    a. Use some of the concepts from chapter three, Asking for Referrals. The important thing to keep in mind is that you always need the customer "confirming" that you are doing a great job. When they say, "We are really happy with everything thus far." You immediately need to plug whatever it is you are trying to do. You should respond, "Great! Since you think we are doing a great job with XYZ, when can I get a chance to help you with ABC?"

    b. Come up with a pilot offering that you can use to entice your customer to give you a shot. Perhaps you can offer free shipping for ninety days if your customers will open their purchases up to whatever product you are trying to push.

    c. Use testimonials from your existing customers that are purchasing the product you are pushing. Get these testimonials in front of your challenging customer. You can also have your existing customers actually talk to the challenging customer; they can tell the challenging customer how happy they are with you and your services.

8. My accounts use me for quotes but take forever to buy.

    a. Set boundaries. You first have to ask yourself why you have been allowing yourself to be used as a quote machine. If you appear to have nothing else better to do than put together quotes, then your customer will continue to abuse your time.

b.   Qualify the quote or project before you put forth the effort. Find out when the project is kicking off and who is ultimately responsible for pulling the trigger. This is where you really have to press the customer. You have to respectfully be forceful with him or her so that you have a clear understanding of when the quote can turn to an order and who is the real decision maker. Once you have the understanding, then you can rattle his or her cage if he or she doesn't hold up with his or her end of the bargain.

c.   Entice these accounts to cut the purchase order more quickly than they normally would. Give them Net Sixty terms (60 days to pay their invoice) or free shipping or a similar promotion for any large quotes that they can turn around in X time frame.

9.   My customer is too demanding.

a.   Have specific time slots in your day or week that are purely dedicated to this customer. Let him or her know that you value his or her business so much that you want to provide a particular time to iron out orders, issues, and questions. Tell this customer that you want to give him or her personalized service, and you can only do this by having one or two dedicated times to talk during the week. Also let him or her know that you will address any voice mails and or e-mails during this dedicated time. This will make the customer feel special, and also it will take the steam out of a lot of his or her emergency issues.

b.   Fire the customer. Let him or her know that you value his or her business, but unfortunately you don't feel that you can provide the level of service he or she is looking for. Use a polite but honest tone, such as, "Unfortunately I see no other way around it. I don't want to lose your business, but I am having challenges working with your account. Unless you have some other idea, I am going to need to close your account."

Before I close this chapter, I want to make something very clear: in no way am I saying to take advantage of your clients. If you have a cordial and respectful working relationship with your clients, you should value this and bend over backwards for them. What I am saying is that you will come across accounts that are, quite frankly, disrespectful, and without a doubt they will take advantage of you. When something like this happens, you have to ask yourself if you enjoy working for free or under minimum wage. I have seen these types of accounts time and time again in my career. You do everything you can to provide value and offer excellent customer service, and the client is rude, disrespectful, and selfish. These sorts of accounts don't realize that every time they make unreasonable demands and abuse their vendors, they are only hurting themselves. Unfortunately, when you play with fire, you will get burned.

I have seen accounts that would constantly beat their reps up on price and make them put together numerous quotes for the same project, only to give it to the competition. They have the rep jump through hoops and do all of the legwork for the quote, only to take the quote and give it to their incumbent vendor. All that the incumbent had to do was simply enter in the part numbers and come back with a lower price. For accounts like that, what goes around comes around. At some point, the incumbent won't have stock and the account has no choice but to go to the rep that they have been taking advantage of. It doesn't take a rocket scientist to figure out what happens when that occurs.

Everyone has problematic clients. Best-practice sharing is a great way to come up with ideas for challenging areas you encounter on a regular basis. If you don't have a regular sales meeting to discuss different ideas, you may want to get together with a group of your peers and have a working lunch. Use the power of people to help you come up with new ideas about solving your everyday challenges.

13

Memoirs from Morty: In Gray Hair, Wisdom You Will Find

The year was 1992. The man was middle aged with a polite arrogance that one couldn't help but notice. After a somewhat rocky introduction, we agreed to disagree on each other's views. What happened next changed the course of my life. Rather than walk away and label me as a young lad that still had a lot to learn, this individual extended his hand and said, "You have the will, but your delivery is off. Have a seat and let's talk." Over the next fifteen years, I have learned more from this individual than any Harvard business course could possibly offer. The next few pages will highlight a few of the areas that you may not find in conventional teachings. Think of them as street smarts for the white-collar world.

Before we dive into the word from the street, I think it's best that I lay a loose foundation to establish credibility for this individual. His name will remain confidential, but his teachings speak for themselves. We will call him Morty.

First and foremost, Morty is a self-made millionaire. He was brought up in a blue-collar world and had to fend for himself at an early age. In spite of financial hardship, he was able to finish school and obtain his degree. This was an accomplishment in itself. In the mid 1970s, Morty went on to become a conventional sales professional and did very well for himself. His earnings were in the neighborhood of fifty thousand dollars a year in 1978. Not too bad for a kid that put himself through school and went out on his own. After working in the usual sales arenas, he decided that he wanted to go into business for himself. While the initial drop in pay may have been drastic, he felt that it was the best decision over the long term. His true passion was building and carpentry. Some thirty years later, Morty is doing great, and his business is thriving. What started out as a few small moonlighting jobs on the side has now turned into a multimillion-dollar business constructing hotels and office buildings. He treats his employees with respect and has mutual respect from the community. Morty has found success, in every essence of the word.

Lesson One: The First Person Who Talks, Loses

How many times have you heard someone say, "Don't talk yourself out of the deal"? Well, take that philosophy and apply a literal meaning to it. The first person who talks, loses. Obviously we use our own judgment for different scenarios, but the general idea is shut up and don't blow it. Here are a couple real-life snippets from Morty that he used to better explain this rule:

During a lengthy sales campaign, Morty finally got his foot in the door for a large account that he had been prospecting for quite some time. After going back and forth on proposals and revisions, he went into the client's office with his final proposal. It was a competitive situation, but Morty had done a good job of proving his worth and keeping the customer's best interests in mind. While sitting in the client's office, Morty handed him his final offering and sat back in his chair. He didn't say another word. There were about thirty seconds of silence that went by, and the client still hadn't said anything. Morty didn't waiver. He still sat there silently and didn't say a word. Keep in mind that this was back in the '70s when it was still acceptable to smoke in an office setting. Morty took out a cigarette, lit it, and smoked the entire thing without saying a word. There had been around four minutes of dead silence without a single word being said. The client leaned forward in his chair and signed the paperwork. Done.

Think about the possibilities for this to go south. I have been in numerous meetings where the sales rep should have taken this advice. In general, people have a difficult time with uncomfortable silence. In the above situation, what more did he need to say? Nothing. He had put his final proposal in front of the customer. It was now in the customer's court to engage. Had Morty said, "What do you think?" would it have really mattered? Maybe, but maybe not. Why bother with small talk when there was no need for small talk? The first person who talks, loses. He could have said, "Do you have a more attractive offer from a competitor?" but he didn't. He could have said a number of things, but he didn't. He kept quiet because there was no need to say anything. The cards were on the table, and the moment of truth had arrived. It was up to the customer to dictate what Morty's next response should be. The client could have felt the pricing was fair, but he needed to figure out a way to get it financed. If Morty had spoken up about lowering the price, he would have only been hurting himself. Morty left it up to the client to make the next move. In this case, the next move was him signing the contract.

The second example takes the rule and adds a little room for amendments and polite humor. It is the same scenario as above, but with a touch of polish. The client was a large organization that had been giving most of its business to a competitor. The deal on the table was not large enough to break the bank if it didn't go smoothly, but it was a great foot in the door to earn long-term business. Upon submitting the proposal, Morty sat back and waited. The client also sat back and waited. The client actually leaned back in his chair and stared at the ceiling for several minutes. Leaning forward in his chair, the client got ready to sign the paperwork but stopped his pen about an inch over the paper. He simply sat there with his pen hovering in mid air. After a few seconds, Morty simply said, "Sometimes that pen doesn't always write, but if you shake it, it writes every time." The customer signed the deal.

So what can be learned from these two stories? Keep your mouth shut and don't talk yourself out of a deal.

Lesson Two: Fear and/or Revenge Drive Buying Decisions

While at a cocktail party, Morty introduced himself to a prospective client who had partnered with his competitor for many years. His intentions were to simply get his name out there and test the waters for any interest. Morty suggested that the prospective client allow him the opportunity to review the building plans for his company's upcoming project. Perhaps Morty could offer up some advice and maybe help him shave some dollars off the bottom line. The client agreed.

During the meeting, Morty noticed a couple errors with the blueprints. Instead of discrediting his competitor with malicious intent, Morty took a more classy approach. He simply said, "I could be mistaken, but it appears to me that these plans are exposing your building to architectural risks. From what is printed here, I am fearful that you may have some structural inadequacies when the final product is complete. In addition to this, now that I look more closely, I have some concerns with the exterior layout and its effectiveness with your business model. It seems that the overall functionality may not work for what you want to do. From a cosmetic aspect, it may not give you the feel you are looking for. You may want to take a look at some of their similar projects and see if you like the overall appearance. I would also ask them for further clarification on the architectural soundness. Again, maybe they know something I don't, but I would definitely check it out."

The client did in fact do his homework, and believe it or not, Morty was accurate in his assumptions. This created fear in the client that his existing builder might have been putting the company at risk. In all fairness, they re-bid the job. Morty came in several thousand dollars higher than his competitor and still won the bid. He knew that his assumptions were correct because he was a professional and could clearly see that the blueprints were off. He won the business because he did an excellent job of creating fear.

Lesson Three: Revenge Is a Bowl Best Eaten Cold

Being able to recognize opportunities to create fear is one thing. However, if you can motivate a buyer by capitalizing on their need for revenge, then you have made it to the Hall of Fame.

Before owning his own contracting business, Morty was a successful sales rep in the agricultural industry. He would sell feed and supplements to large distributors who would in turn sell the product to farmers and other end users. As with any other industry, competition was fierce, and there was no such thing as an easy sale. Morty had been calling on a certain distributor for about a year. He would make his rounds, but he never seemed to get anywhere. Everyone called him by name, but he was having difficulty finding a weakness in his competitor. His competitor was very well known in the industry, and in reality, it was a great company. There was really no glaring weakness that stood out.

One day when Morty was walking the warehouse floor, he noticed a plant manager cleaning up a spilled bag of feed. When Morty asked what had happened, the plant manager responded, "These delivery drivers are really starting to get on my nerves. Sometimes I think they drop these bags on purpose just so they can get paid to clean them up. This time I have had it, and I figured I would clean it up myself." Morty didn't say anything; he just listened. The plant manager went on to vent about the drivers for another five minutes or so. Morty said his good-byes and went on down the road. He called his boss and asked if he would be willing to pick up the freight charges for this particular account if it meant securing the account long term and also getting the main competitor out of the picture. Because this was such a large account, and Morty's company owned its own fleet of trucks, the boss quickly agreed and told Morty that he had his blessing to offer up a deal. Morty went to the distributor's corporate headquarters and secured a meeting with the VP of Operations. In the meeting, Morty quickly cut to the chase and blatantly said, "How would you like to stick it to your delivery drivers and get them off your payroll?" The VP was intrigued and asked for more information. Morty explained that his company owned its own trucks, and they would be willing to take over all deliveries if the distributor agreed to move all the business over to them in return.

They firmed up the deal the same week, and a perfectly good, reputable supplier had been kicked to the curb through no fault of its own. Morty recognized an opportunity to capitalize on the human emotion of revenge, and he knocked it out of the park. The distributor's dislike for the delivery drivers was so extreme that it willingly severed ties with its long-term supplier and gave the business to Morty. Furthermore, the long-term supplier had nothing to do with the delivery drivers. It just so happened that Morty's solution eliminated the need for the drivers, and his competitors were reliant on the delivery drivers.

And what can we learn from these two examples? Plenty! If a person can harness fear and revenge, they are almost guaranteeing themselves success. The trick is to do it with respect and professionalism. When human emotion becomes involved, it is no longer a fair game. The odds favor the one that is capitalizing on fear or revenge. If you do it without respect or in unfamiliar surroundings, then you are most likely going to fail. You have to bring your "A game" to play in this arena.

Morty loves to tell stories about the people he respects. He was very fond of one individual and shared some secrets of his success. This person was another self-made millionaire who made his money selling not what people needed, but what people wanted. I will write it again: The man made his millions selling what people wanted.

Back in the late '50s or early '60s, this individual was driving down the road on his way to run some errands. He had made a few dollars working conventional jobs and was a relatively young gentleman. While on his drive, he noticed a huge banner that said "Grand Opening!" He also noticed that the crowd was enormous. There were cars and people everywhere. The man kept on driving, but he couldn't help but wonder what all those people were doing. It intrigued him so much that he turned his car around and went back to look. What was this "Grand Opening," you may ask? It was a coin-operated Laundromat. The gentlemen secured a loan and opened his own Laundromat that same year. After a few years, he had accumulated forty-six Laundromats. He sold them and retired. This was the first time he would retire.

While killing time spending his hard-earned money, he took up flying. One of his friends called him up and offered to pay his gas, lodging, and other expenses, if he would fly him out west to review a potential business offering. While in flight, he discovered this new concept called cable TV. The idea intrigued him, and he came out of retirement and brought cable TV to the Midwest. His capital gains tax was well into seven figures.

These are just two of the stories that Morty has shared. But the most important part is what we can learn from them. Sell people what they want! This individual didn't come from money, and he made all of his cash by making smart decisions. He sold people what they wanted. If your primary product is a coal-burning furnace for residential housing, I think it is a fair assessment that you aren't going to sell a lot of furnaces. If you are an entrepreneur or work in corporate America, make sure you are selling something that people want.

Lesson Four: A Faint Heart Never Dated a Pretty Lady

By now you are probably thinking the same thing I was when he shared this with me: what could this possibly have to do with sales and success? Well, it may in fact be one of the most impactful pieces of advice he has given me.

When Morty was younger, he enjoyed his freedom and always had beautiful women to accompany him. Now that I think about it, not much has changed in the present day. At any rate, Morty had a way with the ladies. One day while at a convention, one of his peers was having some fun and asked him how someone like Morty could possibly gain the interest of a beautiful woman. Morty responded in kind, "Hey, life is a game of sales. If you never ask for the sale, you will never get the sale. I ask for the sale. A faint heart never dated a pretty lady, and a faint heart never closed a big deal. I simply ask for the date."

How easy is that? How many times have you heard a sales rep say, "Well, I don't want to bother them" or "I hate to seem too pushy"? But when you are busy worrying about being too pushy, Morty is taking your business! Ask for the sale! What do you have to lose? Absolutely nothing. Ask for the sale, and you will be surprised by what happens. Ask for the meeting, ask for the referral, ask for feedback; just ask.

Morty's style may not be for everyone, but it works for him. He has proven himself successful over time, and he continues to grow his business year over year. I suggest that you take some of his concepts and tweak them so that they work for your particular style. He basically has these four previously mentioned areas that he views as fundamental components that drive successful sales. Maybe all four aren't for you, but perhaps one or two can give you a boost.

14

Don't Take My Word for It; Take Theirs!

I thought it would be good to offer up some ideas from neutral outside parties as to how they approach their day when it comes to selling and also how clients make decisions to partner with a sales rep. The next few pages highlight interviews with customers and sales reps and anonymous surveys. As I have said time and time again, it is important to take the concepts from this book and simply apply them to your own style. Hopefully the upcoming interviews will give you an even stronger foundation.

I have taken three customer interviews and included them for your review. The questions were posited to help us better understand what the customers are thinking when they are making a buying decision or bringing on a new relationship. The questions were written with the intent that they could be applied to almost any industry. The main thing to keep in mind, regardless of industry, is that for the most part, success means bringing on new clients. Hopefully the below questions will help you position your particular offering appropriately, depending on what level you are working.

Tom—Materials Management, Two-Hundred-Bed Hospital, Seven Clinics, One Hundred Providers

Q). What do you look for when selecting a vendor/partner?

A). I look at books of business or specific areas of expertise from the prospective partners. They need to offer value to whatever it is they are selling. It helps if they can show me something as to why I would *want* to buy from them as opposed to just wanting me to buy from them. Some of it is driven by contracts (buying groups), price, and quality. Low price does not mean it will be acceptable; quality of product is very important. Brand preference sometimes plays a role, not always but sometimes. In the healthcare industry, you will find that some manufacturers market to the professional to create brand loyalty. They will target a medical student with free instruments while he or she is in college, and then naturally the future doctor will want the brand he or she already feels comfortable with. Sometimes it's just done this way because they play at the top of the organizational chart. Some companies have eliminated the competition because they simply took the mind share early on. Medical school is a place where people start marketing. They get trained in college and then use the same brand in their professional career.

Q). What is the best way for a new partner to get its foot in the door?

A). I have built-in buffers; I don't answer the phone 95 percent of the time. I get a lot of unwanted e-mail. If I don't recognize the company name, I will delete it. The best way is to make an appointment to see me face-to-face. Get something in front of me. Use conventional mail, not email. I hate voice mail. Use regular letters of introduction; maybe include a picture. "I'm new and would love a chance to talk to you." Just be up front and honest; let me know what you are trying to do. Show value. I need to trust you as well.

Q).What causes you to terminate a relationship with an existing partner?

A). Poor customer service. Anytime something is done that is dishonest or illegal—something so stupid that it is a blunder. Going over peoples' heads or contacting other people without permission, contract issues, or pushing too hard. If I don't trust you, I will most likely not buy from you. Trust is a very big component of my relationships. Other reasons are bad mouthing competitors, providing bad customer service, and not being able to deliver. I don't like it when I call a company on Monday morning at 8:00 AM and still get the weekend voice mail. It shows that the company doesn't pay attention to the little things. Things like "That is not our policy" cop-outs and not going the extra mile will also cause me to terminate a relationship.

Q). How important is it that sales reps sells themselves over their company?

A). The salesperson comes before the company he or she represents. I think the order goes the product, the salesperson, and then the company. The product quality has to be there. In my industry, I can't sacrifice product quality. After product quality, the salesperson has to prove he or she is trustworthy and workable. The salesperson needs to sell himself or herself before he or she sells the company. I saw this firsthand before I came on board with my existing role. Early in my career, I went to twenty nursing homes to talk about putting together a food contract with a group-buying contract. This would have saved a considerable amount of money for all involved parties. What I found was that the nursing homes didn't care about saving money if it meant that it would sever the existing relationships they had with their current salespeople. They were that loyal to their reps.

Frank—Director

Q). What do you look for when selecting a vendor/partner?

A). I like to do business with people that use our products and/or sell our products. Coupled with this, I look for aggressive pricing and strong communications skills from my sales rep. It is important to me that my sales rep keeps me informed and is professional in his or her approach.

Q). What is the best way for a new partner to get its foot in the door?

A). Again, it helps to use our products or sell our products. If this isn't the case, then the partner will need to lead with very aggressive pricing in his or her pursuit. He or she also needs to balance his or her approach and not come across as pushy or annoying. If I have someone calling me repeatedly and they become annoying, it will do more harm than good.

Q). What causes you to terminate a relationship with an existing partner?

A). A drop-off in our product sales or a significant increase in pricing will cause me to end the relationship. Again, pricing isn't the key element, but I have to make sure it is fair. If a partner becomes too comfortable and the prices begin to creep up, I have to address these sorts of issues. It would have to be a significant price increase. I can't stress enough the importance of doing business with people who do business with you. If I were a sales rep, I would look for a way to establish synergies between my company and the new prospect. It just makes sense to give business to someone who is doing business with you.

Bob—CIO

Q). What is the best way for a new partner to get its foot in the door?

A). It is very hard to manage a lot of vendors. We like to deal with two or three at the most. Once in a while, we have to bid items out to keep everyone honest if it is a large enough purchase. We have to show management that we are doing our due diligence to get the best offering for the company. It is honestly a timing thing. If they stay in front of us and are respectful of our time, we will give them an opportunity when one presents itself. They just need to be patient and professional.

Q). What causes you to terminate a relationship with an existing partner?

A). If there is a lot of turnover and poor customer service or a significant price increase, I will terminate a relationship. We left our last two vendors because they were changing our sales reps every time we turned around. They new reps weren't familiar with our account, and the customer service fell off. In addition to this, we found out that one of our vendors was charging almost 20 percent more than what their competitor was offering. We will leave existing relationships if there is a significant drop-off in customer service or if we see a large price discrepancy. If pricing is okay and customer service is acceptable, then it is simply a matter of timing and persistence by the competitor.

When one looks at the customer input, what can be drawn from the information? To me, it shows that professionalism and persistence are key qualities. Furthermore, when these are bundled with personal credibility, one's chances for success increase drastically. Clients may purchase products, but they value the relationship the most. I hear sales reps blame their poor performance on a lack of resources or marketing materials. It would be great to have a way to measure how much they actually try to sell themselves as opposed to their company. Think about it: the customers say the biggest thing that is important to them is the overall relationship, customer service, and price. What does that have to do with features and marketing fluff? In my opinion, good sales reps simply need to sell themselves and provide excellent customer service. They may need to use low pricing early on, but in the end, the relationship and customer service will secure the account.

Now that we have seen the customer's side of things, let's take a look at what some of the top sales reps do to increase business. I spoke to three reps from various industries to see what they do in order to increase business. Remember, regardless of industry, our goal is to always be increasing revenue and profit. Here is what they had to say:

Interviews with three experienced sales professionals

Rick—Realtor

Q). How do you approach breaking into new accounts/prospects?
A). The first thing is the mental preparation of setting myself so that I approach them as if they are an old friend. I talk about the need to be able to trust people they are dealing with, and then I smother them with service. I am friendly, upbeat, and jovial. I want them to like me, and I want them to feel they can trust me after one meeting. My intent is to under-promise and over-deliver, but I sometimes promise a lot depending on how I feel things are going. I almost always enjoy

this process, and that attitude helps. If one is in a hurry, it is not a good time to sit down and listen the way one should.

Q). What do you do when a prospect continues to tell you no?

A). Generally speaking, I categorize buyers and sellers into three categories: A, B, and C.

Buyers and sellers in the A category are ready to go now. They are making plans, and they are serious about the services they are seeking. They may be calling you because of a bad experience with another vender or because they really want to give me/you a shot, but hopefully they call because you have moved them in some fashion. The bottom line is that, in my opinion, you shouldn't read anything into why they are calling; just sell them! This is the part where you shouldn't/can't take these things personally in any way, shape, or form. The moment that happens, you become less effective. Believe me in one thing, the customer notices when your approach or demeanor changes, especially if you are defensive, offensive, or quiet where you normally would not be. I never expect a no from these people once I built the relationship. I would expect contact with these folks more then two times per week, and in some case many more.

Folks in the B category seem ready, but they never seem to pull the trigger. They may have a commitment with another vendor, or "politically" it would not be good for them to be seen dealing with you. Again, this cannot bother you, just know what you are up against and move on. It is easy to get frustrated with this type of person, but the one who remains patient and continues to shower him or her with service and updates will eventually get a sale. These folks need to be kept on a mailing list or occasional call list and kept current with e-mail when possible to ease the burden for you. I would expect contact with these folks two to four times per month depending on what I have that might interest them at any given moment.

Buyers in the C category will do something sometime, but who knows when? I like to keep these folks on a mailing list and have information ready when they contact me. This is a great prospect for mailings and special promotions that might get them off the fence.

The only reason these folks are on my list is because they have contacted me. Keep that connection, no matter how weak.

Q). What do you feel are the best ways to increase your monthly sales numbers?

A). Personally, I don't worry about sales numbers except for the number of deals I am doing. If I am able to do enough good for enough people, I won't have to worry about myself. Know that everything we do in life is done with and through others—everything! My approach is to give myself a three-legged chair to stand on. The first leg of the chair is for them to know they can trust me. The second leg of the chair is for them to know I will do what I say. The third leg of the chair is for them to know I will put their interests ahead of my own. Once the chair is built and they are sitting down, you know they are listening. I always feel good about making the sale if I can somehow sit down with someone face-to-face. All I need is an opportunity. Once I have created the opportunity (this is the hard part), the sale is generally easy. Then, as these concepts play out, growth in numbers will come. Once your plate is completely full, do not drop the smaller customers that got you where you are. This is where you duplicate yourself and move on and continuing to add to your customer base. The key at this point is finding someone who you want to represent you or through whom you would be willing to duplicate your efforts. I'm not a sales manager and cannot offer an opinion with any weight from that perspective, but the closer we feel with any situation or client, the more at ease we are with that situation or client and the better the results.

Matt—Technology Sales

Q). How do you approach breaking into a new account/prospect?

A). One of the keys I use to break into a new account is to educate myself as much as possible on not only the company but the individual I'm meeting with. I try to get to know his or her business before I set up my first meeting/call (i.e., locations, key contacts, CIO, CEO, CFO, competitors, and stock info). I will simply learn as much about his or her business as possible. It's a good idea to Google the contact you're meeting with. Get to know his or her background, such as past jobs, education, and other history. All this will show the person you're meeting with that you did your research and actually put some time and effort into preparing for this meeting.

Once I've educated myself, I make sure to have a purpose to my call. I'm not a fan of "calling to check in" or "calling to introduce myself." Typically the people I'm calling on have very busy schedules and get numerous calls everyday. I want my first call to give them a reason to meet with me. In a very vague way, tell them what you have and how it can help them. Get them to say yes. Mentioning an industry hot topic is a good way to catch their attention as well (i.e., business continuity, disaster recovery, decreasing their total cost of ownership, the Sarbanes-Oxley Act, or HIPPA.

After you've succeeded in your first meeting, don't be afraid to ask for referrals. This is a great way to get deeper in the account. As an example, if you're meeting the person responsible for storage, ask him or her for the name of the person in charge of telecommunication.

Q). What do you do when a prospect continues to tell you no?

A). Being in sales means you need to learn to take rejection. No matter how good you are, it will happen. The important thing is how you take it. When a contact says no to a meeting, don't be afraid to press him or her. Ask him or her why he or she doesn't feel a meeting is necessary. You may not be properly conveying to the prospect why you need to meet. Again, this gets back to having a purpose when you call. Phone calls are not always the best way to ask for a meeting. Try different methods such as e-mails, letters, and drop-by's. If a customer feels somewhat threatened, he or she will not agree to a meeting. Sometimes meeting over lunch or happy hour or even golf can be a good way to take the edge off.

Q). What do you feel are the best ways to increase your monthly sales numbers?

A). There are two main ways that I try to increase my monthly sales numbers. The first way is to expand my products/services into the account. By this I mean to ask for referrals and get others within the account to look to you. Having a "champion" within the account is a great way to get your name around. A champion is someone within the account that will provide you with inside information on what's going on with projects, competition, standards, direction of the company, and similar things. Typically your referrals will usually start with your champion.

The second way to increase monthly sales/profit is to get your customer to trust you as a true advisor. Relationships go a long way in sales. If you can earn your customers' trust, over the long term they will come to you for additional products as well. In many cases, this is when you will start to see your profit dollars increase.

Dominick—Mortgage Broker

Q). How do you approach breaking into a new account/prospect?
A). Of my referred business, 100 percent comes from clients I've worked with, including real estate agents and financial planners. This means my new clients trust me already. Therefore, it takes away the "breaking in" part, as the client is warm to me (not cold) and expects a certain level of service. It is important to our team that new prospects/referrals understand that it's not only about a great deal, rate costs, or similar features. More importantly, the level of service we try to accomplish is one in which the customer will not forget our name and will remember that we can help them in the future
Q). What do you do when a prospect continues to tell you no?
A). Because our clients come referred, I only receive a no if the personality of the client does not fit mine. This does not happen often since I am so easygoing, but it has occurred. So in that case, I ask if I can have someone else in my company (specifically on my team) who has a similar philosophy help him or her. The client says yes 99.9 percent of the time. If it comes down to price, I usually ask the customer what are his or her wants/expectations. Based on that conversation, a resolution is found so that the client is happy.

Q). What do you feel are the best ways to increase your monthly sales numbers?

A). Well, it's daily actions that drive that. My daily actions are what cause those numbers to increase. What are my actions?

1. Perform an annual mortgage check-up to see how the family is doing and if there are any changes in life that would cause the need for them to refinance.

2. Keep a close eye on what is happening with rates. I usually keep a list of ten to twenty clients next to me with a breakeven point on rate. For example, Joe Client needs a 6 percent to save $120 per month. Then if rates drop, sometimes for a couple of hours, I get on the phone and call whomever I can to save money. Most loan officers do not even think of this,but it increases sales,impresses your clients that you're thinking of them, and saves them money. This action usually leads to about a 20 percent return in new clients (ten old clients refinanced; two will refer a friend or co-worker to take advantage of the little blips in the market).

3. Continue cultivating relationships with real estate agents, financial planners, accountants, attorneys, and the like. Sending referrals to them instead of asking for referrals goes a long way. It is the easiest way to have another industry professional become a raving fan and to return the favor—and then some!

All through the above-three processes, I am always planting referral seeds. These are actions that lead to more referrals.

In the end, it's about taking good care of the clients that I have worked with and having the new clients experience my level of service for the first time. Therefore, the sales numbers and income naturally increase without thinking about it. Performing the daily actions leads you there.

Do any of the above interviews give you some new ideas with how you approach your business? Have you been leading with price when in reality you should be selling yourself? As you can gather from both the sales side and the client side, price is important, but it is not the be-all-end-all to the relationship. What I took from the above interviews is that, first and foremost, you have to prove yourself trustworthy to the client and earn his or her respect. It may take time, but persistence will pay off in the long run.

It seems that a lot of people get hung up on price. We can't forget that price does play a factor, but it isn't necessarily the driving force behind the decisions. The above customers said they would change vendors/suppliers if there was a significant price increase. In my industry, a couple percentage points can be a nice uptick in my monthly numbers and it won't have a negative impact on the customer relationship. There has to be a balance in the account.

15

Note to Managers: Mr. Big Stuff, Who Do You Think You Are?

What happens in the promotion process that creates a wall between a manager and a sales rep? Oftentimes, it seems that managers forget where they came from. They seem to get so tied up in making that next move up the ladder that they forget the most important part of their team: the sales rep. I don't want to spend a lot of time breaking this down, but I simply want to throw out some advice to anyone who is a manager or is looking to climb the corporate ladder.

Let's start with accountability. If you are a manager, your team is depending on you to help it push things through and bridge gaps between other departments. Too many times I have seen competent managers simply hide behind e-mail and pass the buck. There are managers out there who work harder trying not to work than simply rolling up their sleeves and helping their team. Be accountable for the success of your team members. If they need help, then step up and do something. Get involved. Don't simply shrug your shoulders and say, "I'm sorry; we need to trust the system." That is nonsense and everyone knows it. Think back to when you were a rep. Did you really like it when you heard that sort of thing? Treat your reps the way you would like to be treated. You tell them to offer excellent customer service to their customers, so make sure you are giving them the same level of customer service.

Part of being a good manager is not being a sellout. I have seen this first hand time and time again. Managers won't speak up and actually voice their opinion with upper management. They can see that the direction the company is going is not one with which they agree. In spite of all the warning signs, they will sit back and let the train derail. It's as if people forget how to voice their opinion on what they stand for. If you can sleep at night knowing you have lost your backbone, then keep on keeping on. But if you actually stand for something and truly want to make a difference, then have enough self-respect to actually do what is right. If you don't agree with the company's direction, then voice your opinion. If you are worried about keeping your job, then you weren't the right fit for management in the first place. You have to be a leader. Being a follower is easy. It seems that, all too often, today's managers are better followers than leaders. This applies to working with your reps and your clients.

I remember when I was working with a phone carrier to hook up a new phone line for my house. Being extremely busy, I thought I would take advantage of their online offering to activate set up. After about two weeks without a phone, I finally contacted the company and asked about the delay. It turns out that they never received my online request. After speaking with the customer service representative, I was assured that my phone would be hooked up and working within a week.

After another week went by and it still wasn't working, my patience had finally worn thin, and I decided to contact a manager. Once I was finally able to get to the customer service manager, he told me not to worry and that everything would be taken care of promptly. I said, "Really? That is awesome! As a matter of fact, that is exactly what I thought three weeks ago. So, with this being said, how can you possibly be so confident in your statement that everything will be taken care of promptly?" I pretty much got the standard response of, "Sir, these things happen, blah, blah, blah." I really didn't lose my cool until I asked him for his direct line and he said, "I don't have one." To say that I lost my composure is probably a gross understatement.

The conversation went something like this: "You are telling me that you work for one of the biggest carriers in the United States and they don't give you a direct phone line? So that means whenever you have a family member or anyone else call you from outside your company, that they have to use the general 800 number that takes twenty minutes to get a live body on the phone?"

He responded, "That is correct sir."

My next response was a little more complex: "I run a call center for a living. I know that you have a direct line. I also know that it is protocol not to give out your direct line to yahoos like me. I also know that there is no way in the world that you have any idea if my phone will really be hooked up promptly or not. Lastly, if your call center is anything like my call center, I have a pretty good idea that you are recording this call for training purposes and liability reasons. So, with this being said, let me help you with your training by explaining how this call should have been handled. This is what you should have said: 'Sir, I am extremely sorry for your inconvenience, and I will do everything in my power to have your phone hooked up in a timely fashion. Unfortunately, I have no direct correspondence with the dispatch center because I am in a call center that is about two hundred miles away from your physical location. Here is what I am prepared to do: I will call my direct manager and see if he can pull any strings with sending someone out tomorrow. In the meantime, if you can get me your e-mail address or a cell phone number, I will give you an update as soon as I hear something. Lastly, I want to give you my direct line, in case you have any questions in the meantime or we do not meet our forecasted deadline. I will be your point person and see this through until it is completed. Again, I apologize, and I will do everything I can to have your phone hooked up this week and hopefully save a customer for XYZ Inc.' But instead of doing any of this, you simply took the easy way out and reverted back to 'we are doing everything we can.'"

I have to tell you, it was probably one of the most satisfying calls that I ever made. I finally got him to admit that he did in fact have a direct line but just didn't want to give me the number. Furthermore, had the manager actually done *anything* to show accountability, I would still be a customer. Instead, I went with the company's competitor.

When working within a team atmosphere, it is also very important to have good organizational skills and open communication. These two areas actually show others that you take pride in your work and truly have their best interest in mind. Take a moment to think about what organization and communication mean to you. Does it mean that you have your desk in order and you always pick up the phone when a rep calls? Or could it mean that you are so organized that you have account information at your fingertips, and you proactively call your reps in order to talk about pending opportunities?

The managers that take an interest in their reps' clients and weekly activity will ultimately rise to the top. The managers that hide behind e-mail and fail to communicate will eventually fall to the side. Getting involved is critical when it comes to boosting morale and creating a winning sales force. One has to have the organizational skills to know everything about anything when it comes to your book of business.

I have been in manager meetings where it was very clear who was on top of their game and who wasn't. I used to have a VP of sales that loved to single people out and drill them about all sorts of information just to see if they were involved with their reps and accounts. He would ask things such as: what is the rep forecasting this week, what is expected to ship, what will invoice, is there stock on the product, where is the customer located, have you met with the customer, and what is their budget? He wasn't doing this to be a micromanager; he simply wanted his people to be prepared and involved. If you can't manage your own part of the world, there is no way you can manage a team of reps.

Being overwhelmed means that you may be disorganized and a poor communicator. You may want to take a look at your e-mail inbox. If you have more than twenty unanswered e-mails for more than a twenty-four-hour window, then you probably need some help with your time-management skills. Obviously if you are out of the office, this rule doesn't apply. But the general idea is that you shouldn't close your day with any unanswered e-mails or voice mails. A response time of twenty-four hours should be your goal. I have seen managers who have an inbox of hundreds of unopened e-mails at any given time. Make sure that you do weekly housecleaning and get yourself back on track. Don't be afraid to ask for help.

In a normal week, one should communicate individually with his or her reps at least once a day. Typically, over the phone or in person is the best way to do this, but if e-mail is all that is possible, then it is better than nothing. By speaking with your reps, you show them that you care about their business, and you also can coach them on a regular basis.

Forecasting is a great way to stay on top of your business and what is happening with your reps. By starting off the month with a target forecast, you will have reasons to call and follow up with the reps during the month. If the forecast is too low, then obviously you should follow up with different ways of increasing the numbers. At any rate, forecasting keeps everyone in check. It prevents surprises. No one likes surprises when it comes to missing a goal. I would typically have my reps give me their expected written numbers and shipped numbers. I would then have them break down the forecast with all of their deals over a certain dollar amount.

Knowing one's book of business is vital to being a successful manager. Not only is it important to have a pulse on what the reps are doing, but it is equally important to have ongoing communication with the top accounts in one's region. Too many times I have seen managers that don't even know where their money is coming from. They have absolutely no idea who their top accounts are or the contacts within those accounts. How can one expect his or her sales reps to grow business if their own manager isn't getting involved with the accounts? A simple thank-you call to your top fifty accounts is better than nothing at all.

Conversely speaking, one has to be careful not to communicate too much. We have all been victims of the weekly meetings that are an utter waste of time. If the number-one goal is to demotivate a team, then make the members attend weekly meetings that are boring and useless. There is a fine line between being a leader and micromanaging. Look at the calendar. If there are weekly team meetings, reoccurring development sessions, and company-wide conference calls happening on a regular basis, then something needs to be taken out of the mix. The idea is for the sales reps to be productive; it is very hard for this to happen when they are bogged down with meetings. Most of the time, they aren't even listening anyway.

For the managers who have an ego big enough that they can't get through the door, let me give you a piece of advice: respect is earned; it should never be demanded. If you have to demand respect, then you need to be in a counseling session addressing your childhood problems. People respect you for who you are. They don't respect you because you are their boss. They may be cordial, but they don't have to respect you. Lighten up and just do your job. Don't get so wrapped up in the meaningless details. If you have a few bad seeds on your team, they will eventually fall by the wayside. Don't go on a power trip and ruin it for the rest of the team.

When it comes to setting goals, make sure you are realistic. If you don't think you can hit the goals you are setting forth, then don't hold your team accountable for something that is out of reach. Yes, I understand that if you're not growing you're dying, but there is some common sense to setting goals. People perform better when they have a sense of accomplishment. Give them obtainable goals, and they will feel good when they hit those goals. This in turn will result in them being happier with their career and, more often than not, increased sales will follow. On the flip side, if they are given goals that are out of reach, they most likely won't even exert the effort to come in even 80 percent of quota. They will be so demoralized that it will start a chain of events that will become a cancer throughout the entire organization. People will be spending more time talking about the ridiculous goals that have been set for them instead of selling. Just be smart.

Lastly and most importantly, don't forget to recognize your team for a job well done. It's okay to be demanding, but remember to offer up praises for someone who goes the extra mile or secures a large deal. A little recognition can really pay off in the long run. Recognition will drive preferred behavior, and it also boosts morale.

Conclusion: See You at the Top!

Life is what you make of it. I have taken many chances and have failed many times. However, I never gave up, and I kept pushing myself to become better. I hope that you can use the concepts in the preceding chapters to help you in your own sales career. More importantly, I hope that you find true happiness on your own terms.

You will discover that once you make a commitment to your personal success, people may view you differently. At the end of the day, it really doesn't maker how they view you. They aren't signing your paycheck. As long as you don't burn any bridges and are cordial in your associations, your co-workers or friends don't really have any bearing on your success. They can become jealous when you achieve a level of success higher than theirs, but you don't have to let that negativity affect you. You can maintain focus on your goals without harming your friends and co-workers, and vice versa.

Look in the mirror. You are the only one who really cares if you succeed or fail. You have to take ownership and do something to better yourself. I challenge you to constantly push yourself and work hard everyday. When you think you have given all you've got, give a little more. Start early and finish late. Be committed to your own success and never doubt your abilities.

Remember: poor is a state of mind; broke is a temporary condition. Winners may have been broke, but they have never been poor.

Buckle up and enjoy the ride!

About the Author

Jim Cross is the founder of The Cross Corp (www.thecrosscorp.com), a consulting and training company focused on increasing the client's bottom line by using proven selling strategies and positioning technology as a tool to increase efficiency.

Cross has spent most of his career in technology sales and management. He started his corporate career in 1998 with a growing technology reseller. Beginning as a corporate account manager, he proved himself to be a successful team asset and became the National Sales Manager of their enterprise sales division in 2001. During his tenure as National Sales Manager, this Fortune 500 Company saw unprecedented growth in their face-to-face enterprise sector, which quickly grew into a multimillion-dollar division. Cross's philosophy was straightforward: focus on the needs of the customer, and success will follow.

In 2005, Cross joined forces with Chicago VAR, JDM Infrastructure as their General Manager. By sticking to his fundamental ideas of customer focus and proactive sales management, his division saw more than a 100 percent increase in revenue within his first year on the team.

Cross has a BA in Economics from Eastern Illinois University.

To obtain copies of *Bacon & Eggs* or to find out more information about individual coaching sessions, guest speaking, and team sales training, please visit www.thecrosscorp.com or call 847-560-0962.

978-0-595-47480-6
0-595-47480-2